ANN BELFORD ULANOV

THE WIZARDS' GATE

Ann Belford Ulanov

The Wizards' Gate

Picturing Consciousness

The 1991 Hale Memorial Lectures of
Seabury - Western Theological Seminary
Evanston, Illinois USA

DAIMON

ISBN 3-85630-539-4

© 1994 Daimon Verlag, Am Klosterplatz
CH-8840 Einsiedeln, Switzerland

Cover design by Hanspeter Kälin, utilizing picture by Nancy; photo of the author by Bobhin.

For Nancy

1947 – 1987

Contents

I. The Wizards' Gate

II. Darkness

III. Arriving

All pictures appear on pages 49-64.

Acknowledgments

This volume is an extended version of The Hale Lectures delivered at Seabury-Western Theological Seminary in Evanston, Illinois, in April, 1991. I presented a short version of Nancy's work at the annual conference of the National Association for the Advancement of Psychoanalysis in New York City, in April, 1989. I am grateful to both institutions for the opportunity to present this material their invitations provided.

I want to thank Alex Rupert for his thoughtful transformation of Nancy's paintings into slides that faithfully reveal the originals.

I am indebted to the Faculty Research Fund of Union Theological Seminary, and to The Ann and Erlo Van Waveren Foundation, and to Dr. Olivier Bernier, its director, for financial help toward the cost of the color plates.

I have expressed my gratitude to Nancy in my dedication. Here I want to thank her husband, Paul, for allowing me to work from the original paintings and for his abiding interest in all that this book represents.

My gratitude to my husband, Barry Ulanov, is deep and sustained, for his practical help in preparing the manuscript and for his belief in this project.

Ann Belford Ulanov
Woodbury, Connecticut, 1993

Part I

The Wizards' Gate

1. Religion and Psychoanalysis

Religious phenomena regularly manifest themselves in psychoanalytic work, but in subtle ways, often difficult to discern. The religious elements in psychological happenings must be looked for. We must be attentive, tuned to their frequencies. We open ourselves to the persistent skepticism of our neighbor and even to scathing self-condemnation when we ask, Did we put the religion there? Is it really there at all? For grace and goodness come in ambiguous forms in the shadows of this world. The great presence of the infinite does not easily fall into the small footprints of our finitude. Sometimes the coming of the transcendent bursts all our boundaries and we float into that liminal space at once so threatening and liberating to our space-time perspective.

What then do we do with the All, the Vast, the Radiance that stands steadfastly behind and through the near and the familiar? We make pictures – primordial images of the primordial.[1] Judeo-Christian tradition speaks of the Holy coming to us – in prophets and kings, through daring women and priests of the sacred.[2] The New Testament tells of the startling stepping into history and time and space of the Holy One who brings all images and religions to an end. But still, we must make our way to seeing who is there, receiving what is given, offering our all in response. Our coming to the One who comes to us is our soul journey and for that we need pictures.

Our journey is always marked by pictures of some kind, images that mark us. Through them we project onto what is there and take account of it. We are, as depth psychology makes so clear, symbolizing creatures, drawn and driven to make images that express our consciousness of self and other and world.

Jung stands out among depth psychologists for his passionate investigation of our religious images. Among our instinctive faculties, he said, is a religious instinct, a consciousness of our relation to deity.[3] This sense of relation expresses itself in God-images that we might understand as the religious instinct's perception of itself, or the self-portrait of the religious instinct. Here we find and create what acts as God within us, within our group, within our religious traditions. By entering these images of the center we climb our own Jacob's ladder toward the transcendent, only to discover that the ladder stops and breaks, and that we cannot reach to God on it. God reaches to us, crossing the gap between us and the Holy from the divine side. That is the never-ending miracle.[4]

But miracles can shock and break us. We need to ready ourselves to correspond.[5] We do that by wrestling with our God-images and the gap between them and the Holy. We get tangled up in paradox: we need our God-images to project ourselves toward God in terms we can grasp, but the images break down and fall apart, unable to mediate the incommensurable. We experience the breakdown of our God-images as an unutterable loss that plunges us into darkness, and yet it is the only way we can be sure to notice what is there. Our images both distort God and help us notice God. Our loss of images feels both like the loss of God and God finding us.

This wrestling forms the link between the psyche and the soul. Through it the unconscious makes itself felt in theological education. Theologically, we systematize the implications of our God-images given in scripture, in exegesis and hermeneutic. We draw out ethical and practical implications for life in the world and in sanctuary. We study the history of communities wrestling in similar fashion, shaped by differing cultural forces. In depth psychology we confront these God-images directly. Jung puts it bluntly: "We need some new foundations. We must dig down to the primitive in us ... what we need is a new experience of God." [6] We can find it in the daily work of psychoanalysis where we meet God as a living reality, as Marie-Louise von Franz says, "who can speak in our psyche. One never knows what God will ask of an individual. That is why every analysis is an adventure, because one never knows what God is going to ask of this particular person." [7]

I have chosen to present concrete material to demonstrate such an adventure, which shows us in a woman's wrestling with death how inextricably mixed are matters theological and psychological.[8] We will see how a gap necessarily exists between them and that we cannot reduce one discipline to the other. Indeed, the gap honors their meeting and uniting as well as their separateness.

If we reduce religion to psychology we get pushed into a narrow box. Psychological theory is just one step removed from living experience and rises out of a very small community of authors compared to the twenty centuries and millions who made and lived by dogma. Reducing all religion to psychological theory is like stuffing an enormous downy quilt into a small coffin. On the other hand, if we reduce psychology to religion, we impose fiats on living people that dictate how and where they should arrive before they have ever begun their journey. We do not then leave the bottom open to ferns of ideas, to slimy frogs and talon-toed beasts to slither up from below. We do not dig down to find new foundations in God but think we know all about God ahead of experience. The soul is cramped by a preordained scheme. The psyche is forced to repress what does not fit.

See, by comparison, Lady Julian of Norwich, who took fifteen years to discern what her visions meant, and St. Teresa of Avila, who prayed in the dark and with a bad case of scruples – a neurosis in religion – for eighteen years before she felt God had answered her![9] These women teach us we must grow our way to truth, and more especially, our own particular way of living in relation to it, all of it, including our problems, "for all religions are therapies for the sorrows and disorders of the soul." [10]

In the case of the extraordinary woman at hand, wrestling with the religious issue meant wrestling for life in the face of death, wrestling with paradox until she could touch and talk about religious matters through the symbolic discourse of analysis. The exercise of analysis gave her a voice in facing death's silences and made it possible for her to see the value of life right up to the last. She had something to say and determined to say it even when she no longer could speak. Her death was delayed; she hung onto life until she could communicate with nonverbal eloquence the religious impact of what confronted her. Thus she conquered darkness as she went down into the dark.

Nancy was a woman in her late thirties, just completing a six-year analysis to embark on what Jung calls "the second half of life," when she was struck down by a terminal malignant brain tumor.[11] I focus here on our analytical work which then continued for a year and a half, until the day before she died. Now we embark, you and I, on a joint adventure in religion and psychoanalysis, of a patient and analyst, of verbal and nonverbal communication, of language and picture, of life lived up to death.

2. *Paradox*

We begin by wrestling with paradox. We are all aware in the religious life of the in-between spaces of creative illusion that ritual and prayer create. There the miracle of wine-becoming-blood-becoming-wine of the Eucharist occurs. There we risk open response to the God who confronts us in prayer. We find a similar space framed in a work of art where we can imaginatively experience the suicidal agony of an Arshile Gorky when we behold the bits and pieces of color and shape fragmented all over his canvases.

Psychoanalysis creates a similar illusory space in its sessions. We talk, like painters, about the frame of the work that permits us to establish a space safe enough for a person to experience in transference the inchoate sadnesses, wolfish appetites, fierce angers, and lavish lovings of which we are all capable but rarely fully conscious. The frame maintains itself by the regularity of time and place for the analytic sessions, by rigorous devotion to what the person brings, and a minimal intrusion of the analyst's own personality and problems. The frame is itself an archetypal image of the marking-off of an inside space from an outer one, providing a safe container in which to experience a hard reality.[12]

We need limits and restraint to enter the territory of analysis and to protect the person living there during that fifty-minute hour. If the method of holding the frame becomes paramount the person gets injured. So the first thing the container of paradox shows us is that the limits of analysis will only be broken if they are first put firmly in place and can only be adhered to if they are transcended.

We cannot so construct a method of analysis that captures meanings around the truth it asserts because there is a human person there across from us, looking out from a center of existence. However much a person's center may be dented, damaged, maimed, or even lost, it will burst through any method. Life is not systematic. The center of the human person links to the transcendent, to something outside ego, patient's or analyst's. This center transcends, too, the group egos of family, class and race to which persons belong. It uses the psyche to call us into relation to itself, to our center of self, and to each other.

Jung calls this center the Self with a capital and the journey to it "individuation." Aniela Jaffé defines Jung's notion of individuation well, as our giving "an answer to God – to recognize what He put in us as human beings." [13] Wilfred Bion talks about this mystery as an "O" which denotes ultimate reality. Depending on our frame of reference, we speak of it as God, the infinite, or the thing in itself.[14] We need the method, all our differing methods, to make room for the analytical work.

With Nancy the frame of the entire enterprise broke apart. The length of each session, its physical location in the office, its focus on unconscious materials of dream and symptom, the tensions of transference and countertransference – all were broken wide open with Nancy's first seizure and the diagnosis, soon enough, of a brain tumor called *glioma blastoma,* the worst in a ranking of four grades of gravity, because, as its name suggests, it blasts off, spreading wreckage in its wake. No one with the tumor has lived longer than three months without treatment. With treatment, itself life-threatening, the meantime is two years.

The obvious breaking of routine happened – the re-scheduling and canceling of sessions, the trauma of endless tests, and several brain operations. It was a moment such as Heidegger describes when he calls our basic existence a "thrownness." [15] Like being thrown by a wrestler, Nancy felt catapulted into contingency, knowing death as her nearest neighbor. Nancy felt this metaphysical fact as a daily reality.

A still worse breaking of the frame happened that left Nancy feeling betrayed. The tumor slowly robbed her of her ability to use language, and with her loss of words stole from her her faith in dreams. She had had a large long reach into psyche through her dreams. Truly it was for her Freud's "royal road to the unconscious." In Jungian terms, she knew an unusual connection to the collective or objective psyche. Dreams mediated this other side to her and functioned as her bridge to what transcended both ego and psyche. It is not too much to say dreams mediated to her the unknown as it touched her; they functioned as a God-image. When Nancy no longer could gather what she dreamt into words the bridge was all but broken. As with Jacob, her wrestling with an unknown adversary left her wounded. Her connection to the transcendent was gone. Nancy felt lost, no longer held within a protecting framework.

The frame of analysis then became indispensable. We had to keep the container for the work intact, and Nancy herself created a new frame for her experiences. Both frames, hers and mine, proved durable and gave us entry to do the strong, revealing, finishing and beginning work we did in the last year and a half of her life.

We separated analytical work from all the other kinds of social and professional exchanges that now flooded into Nancy's life – her family, her many friends, countless technicians, nurses, radiologists, chemotherapists, interns, specialists, surgeons, scientists doing experiments. I was only her analyst and could provide only analytical sessions, sometimes in the hospital, sometimes at my office, sometimes in her home, at changing hours and at irregular intervals, for the first four months. Nonetheless, what we did took precedence in her life. In the hospital, for example, we would arrange a time after doctor's rounds and treatment procedures when she was well enough, which was often the case, for she was without gross pain except right after operations or tests or seizures. If visitors were there, Nancy would shoo them out, draw the curtains around her bed and we could go to work. When in the last 11 months of her life the sessions shifted to her house, we set a fixed time every week and adhered to it with little variation. Her analytical hour was accepted by nurses and family as a regular and necessary part of her life, entered into in the privacy of her bedroom. As you can imagine, certain technical and countertransference issues arose, which I will come to later.

Here I want to stress the paradox that the limits of analysis both persisted and broke apart. The limits made the work possible. The breaking of the limits, by life and death, made the work reach beyond itself. We could not reach new levels of communication and perception of existence in Nancy's experience of the infinite except through the durable limits of the finite. We would not have been able to tolerate the intensity of rage, indignation, terror, sorrow for her husband's pain, grieving for a life lost, and the cosmic loneliness Nancy suffered, without the frame of analysis and our willingness to break it.

I took heart from the fact many of the founders of analysis also broke the frame. Freud pounded the couch on which his patient lay, saying, "I am an old man – you do not think it worth your while to love me!" Winnicott bought a patient's groceries and put them in her refrigerator when she was too ill to look after herself. Masud Khan, famous – or infamous – for his tirades, flew to Spain to help the dying lover of a homosexual patient.[16] These actions exceed the limits of analysis at the same time they confirm them. Jung sums up the paradox: "It is a remarkable thing about psychotherapy: you cannot learn any recipes by heart and then apply them more or less suitably, but can cure only from one central point; and that consists in understanding the patient as a psychological whole and approaching him as a human being, leaving aside all theory and listening attentively to whatever he has to say." [17]

3. Background

Nancy was just forty when she died. She had decided to enter analysis six years before her tumor, just after she was run over by a truck and she was laid up in the hospital with a smashed leg, enduring two and a half months of surgery, skin grafting, and painful recovery. She realized there that she was afraid to speak up to her doctors, that she was not living fully as a woman, that life had always seemed "too hard" to her.

She worked two and a half years twice a week in individual sessions, and for four years in group therapy with one individual session a week, and was successfully concluding her analysis when illness struck. Then, after an initial attempt to continue in group, we worked only individually, once a week, for the remaining year and a half. There were three phases to her analysis: an initial two and a half years, a middle four years, and the last year and a half.

Nancy was of medium height (5'7"), very slender, with big dark eyes, suggesting her Italian background, and long straight lashes that she slowly moved up and down.

She had straight dark hair which, in the course of her analysis, she cut and curled into a woolly softness. She dressed with great flair, whether in jeans and hiking boots, or twill trousers and high-heeled lizard-skin shoes, or pale linen skirts with brightly colored silk scarves wound around her slim waist. She would wear a bracelet of feathers, the thinnest of gold chains around her throat, a tiny ivory necklace, delicate hanging earrings. She was a soft, feminine woman, gentle, kind, but also tough. She saw things as they were and always so positioned herself, as one member of her therapy group put it, that she was always in relation to the center, whether positive or negative. This slender graceful woman showed the staying power of steel in her ability to push toward the center, to look and see through to conclusion whatever the center brought. In illness her body swelled to a grotesque shape, her skin browned from radiation. Her hair fell out and she had its wisps stylishly cut to a rakish boy's length. Her face finally assumed the shape of a pumpkin, pained but also somehow amused.

The problems Nancy brought to analysis could best be summed up as a lifelong distance from and repression of ego energies, both of aggression and sexuality. She could not speak up for herself at work, as a scientist in cancer research. Her lab chief would take first authorship on a paper she had written. Nancy would feel depressed; she had to achieve and claim her anger and acknowledge her fear to assert her own authority. She pursued research through *in vitro* experiments which were looked down upon by other scientists in her institution as not theoretical enough, not controlled enough, because you never quite knew after all, what live mice might do. She felt her work was too hard, too isolating and threatening to swallow her life as a woman.

In her personal life, she felt her long relation to the man who eventually became her husband was precious but lacked the important element of passion. She felt cut off from her own sexual depths. As the only girl, oldest of four children, she felt on cordial terms with her brothers, but not intimate. She did remember instigating fantasy games with them in the cellar of her house. Standing high on a box at the pole at the center of the room, Nancy, as captain, would call out to the crew, her brothers, with tales of what she saw on the horizon.

With her parents all was cordial, too, but again without the supporting ground of intimacy to nurture her sense of self as woman. She said, "In trying to get my mother to talk to me it is like throwing energy down a pit. She gives no emotional response." She thought her mother's introversion was her escape from anything that might be coming at her: "She won't own anything and never wants to be where she is. She has a negative voice, opposed." Nancy felt more contact with her father, but not much. "Trying to reach him," she said, "is like mining for uranium." It's fair to say she felt little mirroring from either parent that welcomed her emergence as a girl, as a woman, as a person with her own ambitions, desires, and values. As an adult she also felt unseen by her lover and her lab chief and peers at work.

One person who did really see her was an aunt who lived nearby. She was also central in Nancy's religious history. This sister of her father had her own job, her own interests. She showed Nancy how to sew, and constantly revealed her own femininity. Nancy loved to spend time in her house. Nancy described her aunt as "a shrewd business woman, feminine, religious, a witch." This aunt took her to the Catholic Church and when Nancy was afraid to go with other children to Sunday School, she let her stay on in church through the service. Nancy was impressed by her aunt's devout attendance there, in the service. And then, suddenly her aunt was not there. She died after an appendicitis operation. Nancy was only eight. She remembers no service, no family explanation, no mourning. This greatly loved woman just disappeared from Nancy's life. Later Nancy attended a Congregational Church and liked the pastor as "a kind man." She recollects little else about religion.

She grew up in a small New England middle-class town. She went to college and to graduate school, earning a Ph.D. She did substantial post-doctoral work and earned her living as a research scientist, seeking the cause of leukemia.

Nancy had endured a number of serious illnesses. As a young child she contracted nephritis and suffered many painful treatments for her infected kidneys including intrusive genital insertions. She remembers these as excruciating physically and daunting psychologically – her father felt sorry for the radiologist when she screamed in pain. In retrospect she was angry that no one had acknowledged how hard it was for her. As an adolescent, just as she was leaving junior high school to go to a big high school in the next town, scoliosis of the spine was discovered and she was put to bed again, for many months. When she finally went to the new school she had to wear an uncomfortable large ugly back brace. Her mother said to pretend it was not there and not to speak of it. As a young professional she had trouble with breast cysts, and then there came the accident to her leg.

Intrapsychically, Nancy felt under the domination of a critical "voice," a pressure, a commentator who made her feel "wet, worthless, depotentiated, tired." She saw now that she had felt she had no right to speak up, that she did not value enough what she needed and wanted, that she was trapped in her ardors to try and please others. She called these negative voices "The Wizards" and composed a picture of them called "Wizards' Gate" (*Picture 1*, 10/ 29/80). Nancy happened upon the making of collages in the course of her analysis. Even before she lost her ability to talk, art had become her language.[18]

The Wizards proved effective not by brute force – you will see that the gate has no lock on it and she could walk through at any time – but by invalidating her own plans, hopes, needs, desires, ambitions. They would say, in effect: "Oh, that's not important," or "You are overdramatizing," or "You just imagine that is important," or "Forget that; it will never work out." The Wizards attacked any initiative, whether in love or work. They were real masters of what R.D. Laing calls "mystification," that is, of techniques for separating experience from behavior and thus invalidating the soul.[19]

Jungians would call the Wizards an example of negative animus; they are much more than mere superego pressure.[20] Their whole approach was wrong, getting Nancy off on the wrong foot, making her feel that life itself, not just her work or love relationship, was "too hard." She always had to push herself to do what had to be done. Energy never flowed like water to its source. She always felt her identity as a woman submerged, just a bare possibility, or worse, threatened by the demands of reality. "The Wizards make me an orphan of my own point of view," she said: "I feel I must take an heroic stance to succeed in science, as if I were a man, and that is not my way." One of her collages expressed with humor her anguished feeling that she was always being stepped on by the Wizards. A giant black horse's hoof descended from the sky crushing everything beneath it (*Picture 2*, 11/13/ 80). Typical of Nancy's courage, she took up horseback riding just because the great beasts terrified her. She worked at mastering fear.

For years Nancy lived within the Wizards' Gate, drifting and dreaming. When she had time to reflect in the hospital, waiting for the skin grafts to take on her leg, she realized: "There is more in me to live and to give." [21] She needed to wrestle her way free from the Wizard prison and to enter life.

A basic split existed between this professionally functioning adult woman, independent ever since college, a high achiever in her work, and a dependent, undeveloped part of her which she dreamt of as a fiercely tenacious squirrel gripping her arm, refusing to let go, saying to her, "You must love me!"

It is interesting to note that as a symbol the squirrel conjures up powerful energies associated with the Germanic god of fire and thunder, that it is the emblem of Hermes, the Greek god of transformation, and, in the Middle Ages, was a representation of the Devil. In Nordic mythology, the squirrel was thought to live in the ash tree, Yggdrasil, the embodiment of the world's axis. [22] And so the dream squirrel that digs its claws into Nancy reveals power, the energy to transform what is hidden in her split-off dependency needs. But still, Nancy had to contend with the dissociation of energies symbolized by the Wizard voices, whose terrific energy manifested itself to her only as negative, blighting criticism.

We can hazard that Nancy's not emerging in bold ego terms, but rather remaining stubbornly undifferentiated in dream and fantasy, was her instinctive way of protecting a piece of her true self. It lay hidden in the dependent squirrel to evade the Wizards who threatened extinction.

One of Nancy's dominant transference images of me throughout our work was as a cheerleader – someone excited by and interested in her, in her work, her femininity, her self, her wrestling, her truly entering her life. Naturally the Wizards made fair game of me in this cheerleading role, dismissing me as obtuse, gauche, overdone, or just silly.

Eventually Nancy got angry at the Wizard voices and began to experiment with defying them. Outwardly at work, instead of getting stuck in stubborn resentment, she spoke up, gave scientific talks, published more. She learned to drive. She bought a farmhouse and surrounding land in the country with the proceeds of the settlement of her accident claims, which also funded her analysis. She confronted her lover.

In all of this, her group therapy played a significant part. She was terrified of it at first: how to speak, to show herself, to be herself before others. How completely Nancy joined the work is indicated by what she said at an early session. She arrived late and announced she had seriously considered not coming at all because the group frightened her and she was not sure she liked it. "But then," she added, "I knew I could come here and hide behind the couch if I wanted to, just never saying anything at all. I knew I could do exactly whatever I needed to do or not to do for myself, so I came."

Nancy saw that, to be effective, the Wizards needed her consent. She said: "They evaporate if I am direct." She began to throw off their influence; she was sick of being reasonable; she saw the folly of her father's concern for the technician rather than for herself, the little girl facing kidney treatments. This anger stood her in good stead when, with the brain tumor, she had to undergo so many tests, brain scans, radium treatments, arterio-grams, and experiments with new drugs that threatened convulsions as side effects. The hospital technicians would say, "Oh this will not be too bad, nothing to be afraid of here." Nancy would ask, "Have you ever had this test? Yes, in fact it is very frightening; it is a bad experience." She could speak up and her speaking up made it all bearable for her. No longer locked behind the Wizards' Gate, she no longer felt isolated in her fear. The various technicians and doctors took no offense at her strong questionings but rallied to her as a person in *their* lives. The intensive-care nurses, for example, used to vie with each other to moonlight as Nancy's private nurse at home when she decided to die there instead of in the hospital.

By the time Nancy's illness struck, she had made decisive changes in her life. Jung would call this an entering of the second half of her life, because she was reaching now toward an entire reorientation. After much struggle, she gladly and with great happiness married the man with whom she had lived for many years. That happened in June. Her first seizure struck at the end of the following September.

After fighting for raises and more clear visibility at work, she decided with much searching, and out of her experience in group therapy where she now found herself absorbed in working on others' psychic material, that she would leave research science and take up training to become a Jungian analyst. She felt confidence, even joy, in considering others' psyches and their problems. It did not feel "too hard" to her, but almost like water finally running to its source. She was making applications to schools for the prerequisite clinical degree when she was taken ill.

Her change of careers meant for the first time in her professional life that she would have to depend financially on someone else to support her while she was being trained. Heretofore she had earned her way through gaining grants and her own hard work. This new dependence on others would make room for her squirrel part. Then, suddenly, in late summer, her husband was offered a position to head up a lab on the west coast, and that meant another total change. Nancy would have to leave her friends, her home, her farm and analysis sooner than planned. She and her husband both had planned to leave in January. The tumor was diagnosed in October.

4. Reductive and Prospective Hermeneutics

It is clear that Nancy knew a lot of anxiety in her life, generated psychologically and physically. Fearful questions presented themselves: What caused her cancer? What did it mean? Was her cancer psychological or physical in origin? Such questions cause their own anxiety, and Nancy was pushed to her limits when she asked herself: "What does it mean to get my life really together as my own and as a woman and then to have it snatched away from me? What caused this tumor? Why is it here now?"

Jung puts fear and anxiety in a wider context: "Fear is aggressivity in reverse. Consequently, the thing we are afraid of involves a task.... Spirit is aboriginal and probably always an *agens per se*, and can therefore never be caught in intellectual form. It is a primordial phenomenon...." [23] He tells us to remember: "One's anxiety always points out our task. If you escape it you have lost a piece of yourself, and a most problematic piece at that, with which the Creator of things was going to experiment in His unforeseeable ways." [24]

We are all familiar with discussions about the rival claims of psychogenic and organic causes of illness. To reduce cancer to psychogenic causes alone is to add the insult of moralizing to the injury of the disease. By suggesting that cancer springs from unlived aggressive energies turned destructive against a person's own body, we are trying to assert control over a terrible situation in which we have in fact lost control. Our body betrays us. Health deserts us. Death threatens. But all this effort to protect ourselves only victimizes us. Theologically, it is a flight into an ancient heresy, that docetism where we question the body's facticity. It is a cruel punishment added to an already punishing situation.

On the other hand, to neglect psychological factors in the advent and progress of the disease by asserting that cancer springs only from organic causes, is simplistically to equate life with material reality. Theologically, we are committing perjury against the spirit, denying its real existence. Doing this to others is to ostracize the victims of illness, holding their feelings about and interpretations of their illnesses at a far distance from ourselves because such musings threaten our own sense of security.

The psyche is not so easily quelled – not any more than the body is. In illness, the psyche insists on pushing and pulling the ego into images, metaphors, and mythologies that offer some sort of sense of the catastrophe that has befallen the whole person, body and soul.[25] If we cannot encompass such catastrophes with symbolic interpretations that look both backward and forward, reductively to the origin of illness in the body, prospectively to the meaning of illness for the soul, then we exile ourselves from that creative in-between space where imagination and our sense of God's presence are born.

Psychoanalysts talk about this full-sized encompassing of body and soul as covering traumatic events with our projections – and here we see that psychic projections are not just something we strive to withdraw from objects, but a means by which we can see what is really there.[26] We find and take meaning from a catastrophic event only if we can experience it as part of our "omnipotent fantasy." As Joyce MacDougall, writing about psychosomatic suffering, says: "Only then can the analysand truly possess these events as an integral part of his *psychic capital* – a treasure trove that he alone can control and render fruitful." Then and only then do we accept that each of us is "… uniquely responsible for his *internal objects and his inner world.* The important thing is to discover to what use he puts this inner treasure with its full quota of pain and loss." [27]

Nancy, whose aggression had been so blocked, used all her aggression to make use of her dying. Nancy, who had to work so hard to lay hold of her power and passion as a woman and to confront the inhospitable responses of her environment, lived the last months of her life almost exclusively in the feminine mode. There she was as body, in the midst of, never abstracted from, suffering, communicating empathically more than verbally, still growing a spirit up through the earth. She, the stuff of tubes, medicines, interdependence with others, never separated from any part of her. The spirit incarnated in her and it did not split off from her.

Theologically we know this double vector of symbols through the work, for example, of Paul Ricoeur, who identifies two hermeneutics: The one turns back to archaic origins in our infancy and proceeds by causal sequence to explain the present event by reducing it to its origins. This parallels Jung's idea of reductive analysis: we break down symptoms into component parts that have their origin in the past and cause present problems. [28] The second hermeneutic turns toward the images, figures, and general imaginings that anticipate our spiritual adventure. This parallels Jung's idea of prospective analysis. We ask of a problem where it is leading, to what meaning we are brought through our suffering, to what purpose this problem is moving and perhaps helping to bring about.

Ricoeur focuses on the power of language to conduct us both backwards and forwards. But in Nancy's case, language was obliterated. Moreover, her dreams – her unconscious language – were also cut off from access by the tumor. So Nancy created another language: pictures to convey her sense of catastrophe and of precisely what entered her and what she entered in these dark events – such that, remarkably enough on one hot July day, she could say: "It is all worth it."

Meaning does not come to us in finished form, ready-made; it must be found, created, received, constructed. We grow our way toward it. And sometimes the precious bit of true self, the unlived bit of soul, hides in psychological complexes, in illness, even in tragedy, even in sin. Hence the compelling idea of *felix culpa,* the happy sin that is an occasion of grace. Some mysterious power uses what we see as horrific and as the defeat of all our hopes to bring about our salvation. Jung wrote of his own near-fatal heart attack:

> Something ... came to me from my illness.... An affirmation of things as they are: an unconditional 'yes' to that which is, without subjective protests – acceptance of the conditions of existence ... acceptance of my own nature. At the beginning of my illness I had the feeling that there was something wrong with my attitude, and that I was to some extent responsible for the mishap. But when one lives one's own life, one must take mistakes into the bargain....
>
> It was only after the illness that I understood how important it is to affirm one's own destiny. In this way we forge an ego that does not break down when incomprehensible things happen; an ego ... that endures the truth, and that is capable of coping with the world and with fate. Then, to experience defeat is also to experience victory.[29]

The collision of body and psyche, of the reductive and prospective views, produces, with luck, the answer. Many solutions are possible, but for the individual person involved only one way exists. It is a grace to find it. Nancy found her way, her solution, found grace coming to her. Her wrestling led to entry. Both the reductive and prospective hermeneutics apply.

Paradoxically, we can say that the unlived aggression turned against Nancy and killed her and that she won through her illness, using all her aggression, to the completion of her psychic tasks.

A dream Nancy dreamt a year and three-quarters before her tumor first struck her down can be seen in retrospect to describe the amassing of unlived aggression that proved fatal: In it, she was shipwrecked on an abandoned ocean liner which had run aground on a sandbar in the middle of the sea. She was with four women, all of whom tried but failed to escape by getting a man to rescue them (just as Nancy had tried to get men to rescue her but had failed no matter how she acted to persuade them to help her). A monster had killed everyone on the ship, cutting them to ribbons with a sharp steel disk (slicing into them, the way doctors would describe her tumor cutting into her two years later). The monster was hiding and about to emerge as a bulging in the wall of the upstairs bathroom – threateningly. Nancy found a young black man hiding on the boat. He knew about the monster, but still felt safe where he was, in hiding – alone, reading some very dry but substantial books he had with him (just as Nancy had spent her young years, alone, in hiding, with her books).

At the time of the dream, the image of a ship aground in mid-ocean and of walls bulging with the pressure of a frightening monster made me nervous, but we settled at interpreting the monster in terms of repressed aggression and concluded that she needed to get hold of that to get her life moving. Nancy said the monster was like the

Wizards and made her feel worthless. But when she stood by her "convictions and what she cared about," then she could "depotentiate the ogre." When Nancy was struck by a tumor in her left frontal lobe, I remembered the monster bulging through the upstairs bathroom wall.

Opposed to the reductive interpretation that assigns the cause of her tumor to unlived energy in Nancy, one could say that she used every last ounce of aggression in her illness to emerge as a strong feminine woman related to life and death. She finished with her personal problems of chronic fear and anxiety. She made decisions about her health care, made her doctors consult with her, took charge of her life with her friends, handled her parents with care, and felt at peace within herself before she died.

We might well ask for evidence that in and through her illness Nancy completed the tasks life had set her. I would answer that the proof is in the life as she lived it through to its end. Her accomplishment was a major one, and her illness was an essential part of it, as was demonstrated in the effect her dying had on the living of the people she collected around her. A woman friend, for example, faced the fact that a relationship she had tried endlessly to make work was no good, and she ended it. Another woman friend saw that her business was destructive to her and left it. A man saw that he was postponing the fulfillment of a relationship with a woman he loved and married her. Her husband, who was undergoing his own great suffering in losing her, discovered his true vocation and changed professions in mid-life after Nancy died.

With a great harnessing of her energies and passion, Nancy won through to positioning herself toward the center, so that almost all who came in contact with her felt its effects in their own lives in the most dramatic and concrete ways. For myself, I saw how durable analysis was, that it did not break down in the face of death, that it broke open to nothing less than the infinite.

Nancy's solution involved both Ricoeur's and Jung's hermeneutics, the reductive and the prospective. The illness killed her and clearly, if it had been possible, should have been avoided, and yet the illness took her somewhere she needed to go. That last mid-summer, looking at all her drawings, in one of the few sentences she could still utter, she said again, "All of this is worth it."

Part II

Darkness

1. *The Dark Side of the Self*

To reach peace, Nancy had to go through some very dark times where she could allow herself to join in the long line of questioners symbolized by Job who asks those searching questions: Why does such a terrible thing happen? Why is there such suffering in the world? How can a good, just and powerful God allow it?

In Nancy's case the questions nearly crushed her with rage when her tumor was diagnosed as terminal, unless the experimental treatment she volunteered for miraculously should work. As a scientist on the staff of the institution whose hospital treated her, she was given the best treatment as well as the privilege of reading her protocol. With her good mind she knew exactly what was ahead. But emotionally she could not come to face the fact of death until six months later, when it was clear the treatment was not working.

Nancy's first response was to fight with everything she had and to feel outrage that such things happened – to her and all the other people she met in the radiology waiting room. There they sat, lined up, sometimes until 10:30 at night – children, elderly citizens, women like herself, all waiting to be locked into a sealed room to be shot full of killing doses of radium that made them, Nancy said, see blue flames.

We in religion and psychoanalysis must beware of lining up in our turn, like Job's friends, to give our modern-day version of their explanation – this is happening to you because you disobeyed the Law. In our day we might say it is because your psychological attitude was wrong; you did not live your aggressive and sexual nature fully enough. That answer allows us to evade the horror of suffering and duck the darkest question: Why does evil exist at all? Here evil is the wasting disease that robs a woman in mid-life of the fruits of all her efforts to open up a life and live it fully.

Job, like Jacob, received his answer in the mystery of an encounter with God. God was the author of the Law Job lived by. But the suffering that fell upon Job pushed him beyond the limits of his theology. This God exceeded Job's image of God. Indeed, this God broke Job's God-image wide open.

This is my understanding of what Jung calls the dark side of the Self. These are unavoidable experiences that bring us untold suffering, that cannot be reduced to the sin of fault, to use Ricoeur's phrase.[30] We cannot find a rational causality that will explain and justify those results. Here we find experiences of betrayal, of dying children or hopelessly orphaned ones in war-torn countries, of holocaust or gulag, of psychosis. Such experiences fall outside our images of God; they break apart our God-images; we are left utterly in the dark, forsaken.

We exert our egos to the utmost to throw a net of meaning over such events. We make our exertions, just as Nancy did, to rid ourselves of these sufferings, and we fail. But we hold to what we know of God, just as Job did, until Yahweh showed him something better. Job knew Yahweh as the author of an ethical monotheism, the Law by which he lived, until Yahweh manifested himself in immediate

encounter with Job, talking directly to him. Job then gave
up the narcissism of his point of view – his need to fit
Yahweh to a theory of Yahweh, to the Law that Yahweh
had given him. Job renounced that God-image for love of
the much bigger, whole God who spoke to him.[31]

Jungians talk about such a renunciation as a leap from
the ego's point of view to the Self's, a much bigger one.
The ego as the center of consciousness alone looks at
things from the perspective of the values of consciousness, whether personal or cultural. The Self as center of
the whole psyche, conscious and unconscious, looks at
things from a perspective that transcends consciousness
and may even contradict its values.

The leap from ego to Self circumscribes the radical
difference that comes from seeing things from a view-
point of an ego related to Self, that is, connected to that
which transcends what the ego wants.[32] In religious terms
we speak about this as the excruciating tension expressed
in praying that not our will but the Lord's be done. This is
not to say that the Self in Jung's terms is to be equated
with God in religious terms; rather the Self is that within
us which knows about God and is known by God.

The leap from one perspective to another is also like a
fall in wrestling: the weight of tragedy, the pain of suffering, tears our net of meaning open and our ego falls
through, orphaned. That is necessary when the ego falls
through into the other dimension, that of Self, and must
now look at events from a center that encompasses both
consciousness and the unconscious. We must know now
that we have arrived at the point where our view of events
must include awareness of a greater power. We are not in
charge. Our task is to find a way to relate to this other who
brings us a sense of the beyond, of infinite being, and
even of death.

2. *The Dream*

This task announced itself to Nancy in a pivotal dream
ten months before her first seizure. The dream quickly
caught Nancy's attention, and stayed with her, and proved
crucial in her dying. We used it to navigate a route through
waves of tumultuous emotion. Here is the dream:

> I was skiing along a high pass between two moun-
> tains on a clear sunny day. As I was moving across this
> flat and fairly wide place I heard a voice warn me to
> watch out, I was about to fall off the mountain. I hadn't
> been in any danger but suddenly I found myself bal-
> anced at the edge of the mountain. In front of me was
> an abyss of ice and snow. I was caught at the edge,
> afraid that any movement might send me flying off into
> space. I tried to use my ski poles to lever myself back,
> but they kept bending. Some analytical part of my
> mind was trying to work out the ratio of the snow
> melting to my body-heat and whether it was going to
> become more dangerous to be there with time. I called
> out to the men I knew, but no one answered me. They
> just weren't there. It made me sad.
> Then a voice spoke to me from just behind my
> shoulder. It was a woman's voice – no one I knew, but
> like a fairy godmother – a beautiful young woman,
> more spirit than human. I reached my left hand be-
> hind my shoulder to have her help me get back to
> safety. She didn't take my hand but rather tried to put
> something into it. At first I didn't want what she had to
> give. I wanted to get back from the edge. She asked me
> why I didn't want what she had to give. It was two
> pennies which were also large silver coins. I did want
> them then and was glad she wanted to give them to me.

I knew now that she was not going to help me get back to safety, that she was telling me I had to let myself go and just slip off the edge. I sat there absorbing that fact and then did let myself slip. I had the coins in my hand. I knew I had no choice.

As I started to fall, it was not what I expected. The air was very dense and warm and cushioned me as I fell. I didn't fall fast. The air was so humid it had palpable substance. So I was floating down and it didn't seem dangerous or frightening. Below me wasn't ice or snow but green valley with open fields and some trees. It reminded me of England. I realized it was not going to kill me.

Hearing this dream I made a note to myself. Is this a death dream? I asked. It was the abrupt fall, and especially the coins, that made me wonder about death. Were they a version of passage money to take one over to the other side?

The dream was important and guiding when Nancy dreamt it, and even more so during her illness. It was the one dream she could remember and apply to her terrible awareness of imminent death. In her situation at the time of the dream, Nancy took heart from the central linking figure, the woman who put the coins in Nancy's hands. Only then did she know she must let go and fall. But to her surprise she fell to a new attitude – represented for her by England – not to her death.

In her new situation, facing death directly, Nancy took the dream as metaphor for her whole life. She felt she had had an adversary relationship with skiing because she was "never reckless enough and hence not good at it." It took such a lot of effort. And it was "too cold." It summed up her sense of a life that has often been "too hard." The voice she had heard was that of another scientist, a peculiar man, said Nancy, a kind of hysteric in that he made everything into a crisis, though he managed each time, in the midst of chaos, to survive. "Expect no help from him." She said, "He is like the underside of the know-it-all Wizards."

Trying to rescue herself and failing because of bent poles reminded Nancy of the physical illnesses that had dogged her whole life. Trying to calculate the ratio of body-heat to melting snow made her think of her scientific training, which also proved ineffective now. A completely different approach was needed; nothing her ego had identified with, nothing in her scientific culture, was going to save her.

Calling out to the men in her life to aid her was like her early tendency to wish for and expect a man to rescue her. The dream said once and for all that that was not going to work. She saw that she had been waiting for the man to draw her own femininity out of her and that she did not stay connected to it herself. She expected a man to provide connection to the feminine. When no man did, or could, the revenge of the feminine that she had neglected in herself was to make her feel small and alone.

But here the feminine spirit reached to her. This was the most important thing in the dream to Nancy along with the surprise at dream's end of falling into that green land of England instead of being killed. The feminine spirit had changed everything by communicating a new attitude symbolized by the coins. For it was only when Nancy took the coins, and discovered she wanted them even more than she wanted to come back from the edge of the cliff, that she could let go and fall into a new place.

In her association to the dream when she dreamt it, ten months before her illness, Nancy concentrated most on the coins. They are like a treasure you give a child to keep in her mitten. They have no practical value – mere pennies – but they remain something precious to you, that you cherish – impossibly large silver coins, better by far than prosaic copper pennies. Both copper and silver are linked symbolically to religious and feminine themes.

Copper is a lesser metal, of little worth, cheaply available, though valuable and durable, especially in pipes that conduct water and heat. The word itself is derived from the Latin *cupram* and the name of the Greek island of Cyprus, the best source of copper in ancient times. Copper also derives in some readings from the Hebrew *gopher*, the name of the tree from which the wood came for Noah's ark. In alchemy, copper is linked to the planet Venus which stands symbolically for the warm, moist feminine conductor of beauty. Alchemical procedures transform copper into silver, which symbolizes purity of soul in the individual and in humanity in general, something entirely human, unadulterated by outside influences. In the psalms, the word of God is compared to silver as is the Virgin Mary. In some symbol systems, silver also stands for the moon and the feminine principle and in the philosophical tree of alchemical metals represents the cross of Christ. We see the psyche's power of economy in this little dream detail that offers coins made both of copper and silver. In the making over of copper pennies, of such little worth, into large silver coins of great value, the process of transformation is demonstrated, both of the feminine to become its own pure self in Nancy and of religious mystery in the link to the Ark and the cross.[33]

The coins reminded Nancy of an article she had read about money as a symbol of the Self.[34] She recalled from it that coins as money enable one to live in the hard practical world as a means of transformation from one thing into another. Thus are things often set in motion. Coins also turn up as the fee for passage from this world to the next, payment to the boatman who ferries souls across the river Styx to the Land of the Dead. Coins thus effect transition from life to death, a means of entry to another dimension of being. In this sense money is a talisman of the Self, an object invested with supernatural power which can be assigned to any object, just as through reversal any object can become money. As talisman, money can actively support the Self as it moves to achieve Self's aims.

The Greek word *telos,* from which talisman stems, adds to our understanding of talismanic nature: it can turn, be pulled in and around; it can turn as toward our fate.[35] The coins handed to Nancy in the dream reveal that she must let go and fall off the mountain. She was moved to confront her telos, that which determines our worth and often is projected onto money, as a measure of our worth.

The goal of the dream-ego is to draw back from the edge, to get her back on track, to go in straight lines from peak to peak. The Self's goal, represented by the feminine voice and the coins, is to turn the dreamer round a deeper axis, a telic center that imposes ethical obligations learned in secret consort with the Self. In the dream Nancy is urged to let go to the Self, to let it come in to her. It is our ethical relation to the Self that binds us together as community, as Rusell Lockhart has noted.[36]

In Nancy's dying, her letting go of identification with her ego-values to fall into the Self, had large effect upon many others. She collected round her what might be called a group of "soul friends," those who could withstand the impact of what had befallen her and not force their grief for her onto her. Instead they must reach into their grieving emotions and perceptions to their meaning for themselves, thus experiencing their own fall to the Self.[37] All of us in this small circle, as I have said, felt a great positive impact on our lives in Nancy's death.

Money, it is worth remembering, possesses its own sig-
nifying etymology. It is a feminine word deriving from
Mnemosyne, mother of the Muses and goddess of memo-
ry, source of so much creativity. Money is also connected
to Juno, queen of heaven, at whose temple money was
minted and where she was eagerly sought as advisor and
seer.[38]

Nancy had a positive association with the unexpectedly
warm substantial air that supports her descent in the
dream. It recalled a poem by Gerald Manley Hopkins that
compares the air that sustains us to the Virgin Mary,
emblem of the archetypal feminine.[39] In her we breathe.
In the blue of her cloak we find the blue of the sky. Nancy
in a sense, fell upwards, into the supporting blue substance of the feminine. Could we say that Nancy, whose
feminine nature had been left so uncompleted in life that
it seemed suppressed, found near death a symbol that
bodies forth to her the receiving feminine as she plunged
off the mountain? Could this be one of the meanings
hidden in the catastrophe that was to confront her? In
more immediate terms, after this December dream Nancy
could open herself more fully to loving. She was married
six months later in June.

Alchemy takes us far with the symbolism of the air with
which the sky confronts us. As von Franz puts it, the entire
opus of transformation "culminates in the production of
the so-called *caelum,* the inner sky." This goal or telos is
"the extracted quintessence of the life of the body, the
inner truth which, as God's exact image lies hidden in the
innermost recesses..."[40]

In his commentary on alchemy, Jung takes a similar
path: "The production of the *caelum* is a symbolic rite....
Its purpose was to create, in the form of a substance, that
'truth,' the celestial balm or life-principle, which is identical with the God-image. Psychologically, it was a represen-

tation of the individuation process by means of chemical substances ... or what we today call active imagination. This ... occurs when the analysis has constellated the opposites so powerfully that a union or synthesis of the personality becomes an imperative necessity."[41] Nancy was plunged into the battle of conflicting opposites after her tumor was diagnosed.

Nancy is going to die, but when she falls off the cliff in her dream she is lofted through the sky to a new place of departure. In alchemical terms, the air in the sky represents inner truth or a God-image, and Nancy's falling into the sky links her experience of death to what Jung calls an experience of a mysterious "tendency to spiritualize the 'body.' It represents nothing less than a *corpus glorificationis,* the resurrected body whose relation to eternity is self-evident."[42] Less than a year later Nancy was groping for the spiritual meaning of what was happening to her body. Torn on the one hand between her ego's rage at being struck down by illness and her determination to get well, and facing on the other an opposite view of the Self that saw this illness as part of her task to reach and live out her feminine nature, she longed for a third point of view that would reconcile the opposites raging within her. This could be what alchemy defines as the union of the *caelum* and the *unus mundus,* the world-principle. In such a union we experience our life as "cosmologically meaningful." Jung thus links the psyche's work with the soul's; this *caelum* is "the living stone, mentioned in the New Testament. Above all, its incorruptibility is stressed: it lasts a long time, or for all eternity: though alive it is unmoved; it radiates magic power and transforms the perishable into the imperishable, the impure into the pure; ... it is simple and therefore universal, the union of all opposites; it is the parallel of Christ and is called the Savior...."[43]

Nancy loved England as a "home country." It has "a past," she said, "humor, and a kind, civilized way of life." It represented living life to her. It was a metaphor of return – to the I and to the Self. I was reminded of the famous anthem linking Jerusalem as the city of heaven to England as a green and pleasant land, a symbol of a lovely place of life after death.[44] For we must remember the puzzling conclusion of the dream, so at odds with the subsequent facts, that as she falls, Nancy, the dream-ego, recognizes that "this is not going to kill me."

When the ego is related to the Self's point of view, and views things from the center of the whole, not just from its own one-sided partiality, it knows it will not die. Inevitably, one wondered if this was a task set Nancy in her long day's dying, to see that what was ahead, even in her dying travail, was eternal life.

Jung's comment to a dreamer of a similar dream, where the dreamer was forced to leap from a precipice, is helpful. "Such dreams occur at the gateway of death. They interpret the mystery of death. They don't predict it but they show you the right way to approach the end."[45]

3. The Feminine

Darkness faced Nancy in many forms. Her illness drew a shadow over the light of the life that was just opening up to her. The diagnosis – terminal illness – extinguished the light coming from her self-constructed God-image. Coping with her devastating illness constantly threatened to blot out the little window of light opening to her in her analytical sessions, where she was exploring the meaning of all that was happening to her. Darkness was everywhere about her as she slowly lost her ability to speak.

It was this loss of speech that finally took Nancy's God-image from her. She was not formally religious and never identified herself as such. But in Kierkegaard's sense of Religiousness A, Nancy was deeply faithful.[46] She saw through the seen to the unseen; she reached to the symbolic life and everyday felt its counterpoint of hidden meanings. This allowed her to enjoy the literal sensate life – eating Chinese food, going to movies, art exhibits, walking in the woods – finding in these events the constant workings of fate, a large power which she strove to receive and to honor.

For Nancy the principal means of attending to this larger presence was dream. Dreams were the median of the axis between ego and Self. Dreams mediated the transcendent to Nancy. Working to understand her dreams provided her with a disciplined means of response to the daily stuff of life and the greater center the dreams pointed to. That was what she believed in. She worked hard on her dreams by herself and in her analysis. Together, we turned them around in their vivid centrality.

When the tumor struck and then finally obliterated her capacity to speak, Nancy felt thrown far into the dark, robbed, disowned, betrayed.[47] The loss of speech broke the frame of analysis. We could no longer work dependably through the exchange of words. Speech came and went, and eventually departed for good. Nancy knew what she felt and perceived, but could not put her hands on the right words to convey the feeling, neither in sound nor on paper. It was as if she were reaching into a refrigerator for milk and came out instead with a banana. It was frustrating. It was frightening. I realized as never before how much analysis depends on verbal exchange. I also came to see – happily – that that was not true of the depths of analysis.

When she could no longer rely on words to frame her

feelings, perceptions and dreams, Nancy constructed another version of the archetypal frame for our work. She painted pictures. Together we descended to a more immediate experience of communication, no longer in abstract verbal exchanges, but in a mutual indwelling through empathy and identification in an emotional field. We were not fused, nor merged. The usual method of seeing, analyzing and withdrawing projections did not hold any longer. Now we dwelt together in an interactive field that included body and psyche, ego and soul, and made use of a kind of imaginal sight that is closer to unconscious thinking than to consciousness.

This space is not unknown to analysts or philosophers. It is akin to Jung's space of the archetypal, and Cassirer's level of mythopoetic imagining. Winnicott writes of transitional space and Loewald of archaic mind; Milner of the two kinds of seeing, with the eye that imposes its view and with the eye that sees what is really there.[48] Those concepts helped me. But something more was going on here which the analytic concepts did not deal with, not explicitly, in any case.[49] Nancy and I were facing the transcendent. In religious terms one could say Nancy and I were venturing jointly into the realm of contemplation. We looked at what was coming toward her, and into the analytic task of sorting out all her different reactions to it.

To do this sort of contemplating and communicating we had to draw heavily on a feminine mode of being. Guntrip writes about the "female element of being," using Winnicott's terms, as the *sine qua non* to get our egos started in a personal life, to make our life as persons.[50] Klein writes of the feminine position we all live regardless of sex; Freud, of the bisexuality of our psyches.[51] Jung writes of the feminine as the archetype of life in a man's psyche, and as the great connector and completer of the human psyche, as that readiness to move toward wholeness that we all know in our deepest privacy.[52] In my own writings on the feminine I have described this mode of being human in both sexes as a downward going way which situates us in the midst of our experience instead of keeping us standing abstracted from it, merely conceptualizing it. The signal mystery of this downward-going, opening, entering path of the feminine is the indissoluble union of opposites it brings about, of the spiritual and the material, of the religious and the sensual, of the eternal and the historical, of the abstract and the personal, of the elemental and the transformative.[53] The goal of the feminine mode is completion, reaching out to include all apparently opposed emotions, drives, insights, attitudes, faults, and talents.

The feminine is the real initiator of change to effect inclusion, enlargement, union. This urge to completeness brings with it less a self-consciousness than a consciousness of self – of all of our aspects, our less developed alongside our developed sides, our fears and damaged places as well as our superior functions, our madness and left-out bits as well as our clear achievements. Paradox marks the knowing and acting of life in the feminine mode; we stretch our consciousness to make it big enough to hold opposite emotions without splitting them into either-or thinking, or us-them actions where we must lose our grasp of wholes.

Nancy had a natural flair for such inclusive paradoxical thinking, but there was a tug in the opposite direction through her identification with her father – they were the two highly educated members of the family – and in her post-doctoral work.[54] She had been forced and forced herself into what feminists call patriarchal thinking, which, at its best, marks one of the great achievements of the masculine mode of being. Here abstraction, analyzing things into discrete parts, separating self and other, generalizing from the particular to the universal, deemphasizing one's personal experience as a major factor in one's experiments – all make tremendous contributions to our culture and to our individual development.

But Nancy felt trapped there, behind the Wizards' Gate. Indeed, the Wizards themselves can be seen as caricatures of such abstract modes, invalidating her feminine way of thinking, feeling, doing. Pursuing the scientific career her father had always wanted, identifying with the strains of denial in her mother, following the procedures in the educational institutions and professions she had chosen, she found little support in herself for the feminine modes that were her natural bent.[55] Nancy forced herself into the channels of dry abstract thinking, in writing scientific grant-proposals, leading or participating in scientific discussions. Even so, in her scientific research she could not help making a large place for her wonder before the mysteries of nature where she sought to cooperate not to conquer. When in such spirit she presented her work, colleagues reacted ambivalently. She told "stories," they said, rather than prosecuting scientific proofs. They were captivated, startled, thrown off balance.

Though on the staff of one of the world's most prestigious scientific institutions, she always felt in some way out of things, because her hidden starting point toward science was so different from the established one and issued in such different kinds of experiments. She liked for example, to work with live mice rather than smears on slides. Her work to find the cause of leukemia, always opened onto the indeterminacies of life: you never knew with certainty what fractious live mice might do! Her work remained suggestive rather than conclusive, quite against the prevailing fashion of the institute.

It was this wrong starting point as much as anything that made things always feel "too hard" to Nancy. She did not know in full consciousness that her way was so much at odds with those around her. She needed to grasp the feminine mode working in her, to accept it and use it. That was very difficult – it had been so little mirrored and supported in her life. She held back in her work, knowing somehow that if she gave all of her energy to it, she would be swallowed up by its masculinist modes and assumptions. Protecting her hidden feminine way of being, she sacrificed advancement in her work. The resulting muddle reinforced her feeling of confusion and difficulty. Reaching her true feminine mode of being, of knowing, of acting was the essence of Nancy's work in analysis.

As is often the case with people who have worked from a false starting point, to arrive at a true one usually means a great change in life, and so it did for Nancy. She was newly married, ready to embark on a new profession, about to move to another part of the country. Her illness ended all that, but not her living in her own feminine mode of being, not her journey toward her true self.[56] This was one of the first great meanings Nancy discovered in her illness.

The place of her tumor meant a gradual breaking-down of the left-brain thinking in which Nancy had excelled, at whatever cost to her sense of self. A month after the tumor was diagnosed, all she could make of it, she said, was that "I have to stop dealing with life through my head and use my heart." She soon felt stripped of her old functions. She did not *have* to know the statistical odds of cure predicated by her medical diagnosis and procedure. She sensed now just how much and how little she needed to know and did not feel pressed to ask for more until she was ready for it and it was ready for her. She was stripped of all reliance on the old ways of abstraction and prediction, with their tidy, if untrustworthy certainties. She plunged into her darkness.

(text continues p. 65)

Picture 1 – 10/29/80: "The Wizards' Gate"

Picture 2 – 11/12/80

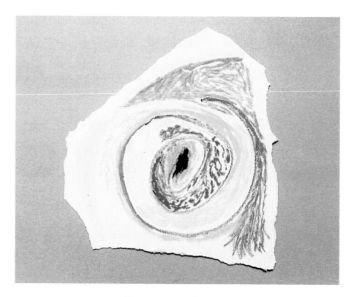

Picture 3 – 2/24/86

Picture 4 – 2/25/86

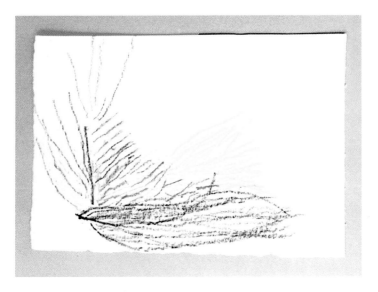

Picture 5 – 3/19/86

Picture 6 – 4/7/86

Picture 7 – 4/7/86

Picture 8 – 5/6/86

Picture 9 – 5/15/86

Picture 10 – 6/17-20/86

Picture 11 – 6/20/86: "Sun Earth Oceans Eternal"

Picture 12 – 6/29/86

Picture 13 – 6/30/86

Picture 14 – 7/3/86

Picture 15 – 7/8/86

Picture 16 – 7/15/86

Picture 17 – 7/24/86

58

Picture 18 – 7/25/86

Picture 19 – 7/27/86

Picture 20 – 7/29/86

Picture 21 – 8/5/86

Picture 22 – 8/18/86

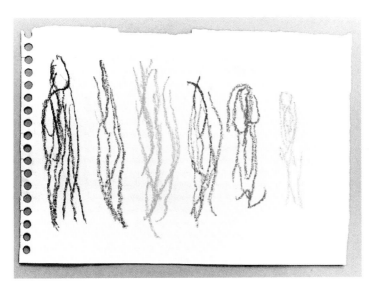

Picture 23 – 8/27/86

Picture 24 – 9/4/86

Picture 25 – 9/8/86

Picture 26 – 9/9/86

Picture 27 – 9/23/86

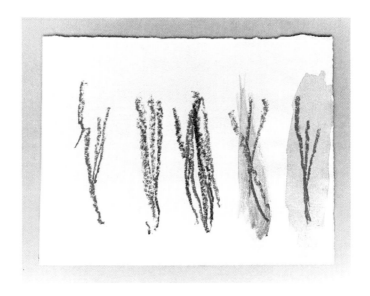

Picture 28 – 10/8/86

She lived in her temporal here-and-now, less and less tied either to the past or future, accepting that mode of unknowing that allows us to experience what we know and do not know, letting us cross back and forth across borders of knowledge and experience. At its best, living in the "eternal now" that death pitches us into is like reaching the being-now of religious contemplation. We behold the existence of being directly.[57]

Depth psychologists write about it as both central to their theories and at its farthest edge. Winnicott talks about living creatively as different from being healthy; Masud Khan writes of an experience of self that transcends the id-ego-superego structure; Guntrip focuses on the mystery of the person as a curing factor; Kohut writes of the self as an essential but still indefinable notion; Jung stresses the ego's task to house the Self-experience. How to live toward the infinite? How to live in relation to it while anchored in the finite?[58] This became Nancy's work in the last year and half of her life.

This work plunged Nancy into direct experience of the opposites in her life. She struggled to house and bring them into relation to each other. She had lost her language; she faced a vast, dark, mute space. She consented to persistent feelings of abandonment and bleakness but struggled not to be overcome by them. The struggle brought out the steel in Nancy's character as she was tempted again and again to turn her face to the wall, take sedatives, and withdraw. She kept to the task of relating to what was happening to her, finding or creating meaning in it. Otherwise the fight would just go on unconsciously and nothing would come of it.[59]

Nancy remained firmly there in the midst of what was happening to her. The change from her usual abstract modes had a salutary effect. She stripped off all the lingering ego-problems that had brought her to analysis in the first place. She no longer feared to speak up but squawked loud and clear when medical procedures frightened her. She was on Jacob's ladder, struggling towards the ultimate. She brought technicians, nurses, doctors into direct relation to herself. Her gentleness inspired affection all around her. Now she no longer had to hold back her emotions. She would cry, get angry, express regret, say she was anxious. She released emotion instead of drowning in it; she felt less isolated. She no longer felt pent up sexually or blunted in her capacity to love. Her love, she felt, was emerging easily, without obstacle, moving directly to her husband. There was nothing they could not talk about. She felt deeply happy in loving without reserve and feeling loved in the same way. Her husband tended her with great care. Any obstacle he had felt also seemed to vanish. Now she no longer feared anger. When at times she felt herself immersed in it again, enraged once more, she knew her self able to express it, with special venom reserved for the hospital "vampires" who always wanted more blood. She made her point with humor by wearing a lurid purple and green tee shirt emblazoned with the message "This ain't no wienie roast!"

Free of her personal problems, Nancy could concentrate on the task of living fully, right up to the moment of death. This demanded both toughness and a playful spirit. At night she and her husband and father would create what she called "mad dinner parties," gourmet bedside meals. Nancy would take tiny servings and a thimble of wine. As late as just a few weeks before her death, her last birthday, she joined happily in the festivity, with ribbons on her oxygen tank and streamers on her feeding apparatus and lovingly received the ingenious present her husband gave her, a small, soft, brown, fuzzy, stuffed bear. She liked to feel its fur with her thumb as it lay on her stomach.

Nancy carefully regulated visitors. Those who could enter this "eternal now," this play space between life and death, this territory where all the opposites collided, keep their own footing, and feel their own feelings, Nancy saw gladly. Those persons who denied that this difficult place was where she lived, could not carry their own feelings, and wanted her to do it for them, she refused to see. Her mother fell into this category, though Nancy did spend some time with her when she showed up. But in general, Nancy said she had too much to do and too little energy to carry anyone who could not meet her exactly where she was and the way she was.

4. Pictures

Nancy hit upon an extraordinary way to face and explore what was in front of her by drawing pictures. This way she could express what she experienced and make others feel it.[60] At this time, she was still able to say a few sentences. Her ability to speak came and went, suddenly deserting, suddenly coming back for a moment almost to normal.

Picture 3 (2/24/86) is one of the earliest that Nancy drew. You will note she drew it on a scrap of paper, a remnant, torn at the edges. This seems to say Nancy felt like something to be thrown away, a life torn in two. The black center of the spiral made me think immediately of the tumor hidden in her head. Still, the bright colors and clearly defined line of the spiral describe purposeful movement toward the center and away from it.

She herself said, "it has an abdominal body to it; it may be nothing, but it touches that center; I wonder if that is true." Nancy drew the picture in February. She looked at it again in April, when she said of it, "It means everything.

It scares me in part. When I first did it I was afraid of it. Now I'm not so sure. Where is this black coming from? I was very frightened... Now it's more than just the dark: it's positive. It's real. I'm afraid of it. It scares me so. What is it? It's not death. It's so big."

Nancy drew *Picture 4* (2/25/86) in February the day after the previous picture at a moment, she said, when she was very scared. She liked these two best of her early drawings. Of this one she said, it is "the tumor with shock waves, and yet with an enduring center in the dark; it has suffering in its jagged lines; it has a black-magic character to it, weaving a spell, yet a funny eye to it, make-believe but real; an Anglican part of me that does not have a soul, so that the soul just becomes born." We talked about the soul as meaning one did not have to carry everything by oneself. After what she had put up with physically – all the operations and tough convalescence – getting a soul would be a cinch. That got a good laugh.

Of *Picture 5* (3/19/86) Nancy said, "the whole thing reminds me of a bee; it goes together and it's waiting." I asked what it was waiting for and she answered that it was "very complicated: the amazing black part holds onto things ... and what makes it safe is that it has the yellow and green. That's what keeps it from being bad: the green and yellow keep the opposites from vying. It's painful."

A bee has a sympathetic system that functions automatically and mechanically, I remembered; it has no cerebrospinal system at all but a ganglionic one that nevertheless can produce thoughts and perceptions. Jung sees the bee as "the symbol of the dormant kundalini that is ready to strike...." Its purpose "... is an intense enhancing of the Self ... individuation ... a greater awareness...." [61]

Nancy suffered an increase of terror as she became more and more visibly ill, with her loss of hair, her skin browning, her trouble walking, speaking, or seeing. She could no longer write or sign her name, yet she could and did manage to draw and paint. By March she was confined to her house and so from then on I went there once a week for our sessions. She was sorting out what was happening to her, facing up to death.

One day (3/13/86) she said, "It's hard. I'm just terrified. Not all the time but certainly some of the time." I asked, "What are you terrified of?" "It's just terrifying." I asked if she was afraid of dying. "Yes, that's the worst." Let's talk about it, I would say, "because I imagine you don't talk about it and then are stuck with it alone." "Yeah," she said, "I don't; very hard." Here Nancy lost her language. Then she said, "It's canny and it's uncanny." Is it leaving life or fear of where you're going? "It's both.... I'm living a lot and I'm not living ... I can't get any meaning to it.... It's goddamned frustrating and it isn't right! On the other hand, I'm not doing badly."

At the next session (3/20/68), Nancy expostulated: "It's rotten ... I'm so beaten down ... It's wrong and I do not pretend to know. I do not know what to do." I said that one thing I saw is that she was mad, with no ambivalence or ambiguity about her anger. She agreed. "I'm furious! It's just too much ... It's bigger than I can stand, and yet it isn't."

I saw that there were two points of view here and she might look at the illness from each one. "Yes, yes, yes ... It's just so cold and rotten." She struggled to find the word and could not. She made a fist. I asked if it was cold as in the ski dream, falling off the cliff. "Yes, yes, and that helps." The dream view, I suggested, offers a way to get off the cliff, because she was really going someplace, into the warm air and green, not just leaving.

The very next session (3/27/86) proved pivotal. Nancy, looking thin, bruised, and brown, started right off: "I'm mad! It's wrong! I'm tired of being tired; it's sickly to

be in this situation. I don't know what to do. I'm beginning to feel bad." She cried, losing her speech. I asked if it
were possible to yield. "I've got to," she said. "I've got to."

I asked if there were anything on the other side calling
her. "Yeah. But more than that. It's taking me somewhere. I feel better saying it. Something is pulling me."
The thing "to do," I suggested, was to look, to sense, to
hear, what was pulling her, even to ask, Who are you? Give
me something. Does it show any colors? "Yes," she said.
"Yellow and gold." Then Nancy broke down and sobbed.
"I don't want to die, I do not want to die. I'm scared." She
cried and cried. Then she said, "It just hits me and I know
that I know about it."

"What is it that you know?" I asked her. "It's real. It's
frightening. But it's also forgiving, do you know? It's a
beautiful place ... It's just lovely," she laughed. From that
point of view, I commented, it was saying, Come on:
enough already! Her laugh, I told her, had a fiendish
chuckle in it. She laughed loudly, happily almost. "Yes.
It's different from the suffering; it's forgiving. The whole
thing is all right."

"How strenuous," I said. "Just big opposite emotions.
This is your work. Like the dream, first fear on the cliff,
and then you receive being held when you fall from it."
Nancy asked, "Will I die from this?" And she cried.

Words were hard, but I asked: "What do you know in
your body?" She whispered, "I think so." I nodded in
agreement: "I think so too."

"I just get scared," Nancy said, "like two things – pulled
by terror and suffering, and then going somewhere; and I
must know about it." That is your work, I told her, to feel
both sides and to know about them and each week knowing more and you telling me about it. "Yes," she said. "It is
very important to tell you because it is very hard to know

and not say; I can't go into that place without you knowing about it." "And so," I said, "leaving is arriving."

After this session Nancy felt great happiness and experienced an outburst of drawing. I attributed it to her
expressing her anxiety openly, strongly, no longer carrying it all by herself. We had marked out the work we had
to do: How to live while dying. All the subsequent sessions
until mid-October focused on her opposed reactions to
death: terror and outrage on the one hand, feeling she
was going somewhere, to peace and beauty on the other.
She asked me to tell her husband the ski dream. I did so
and he found it comforting. With friends and nurses she
schemed to buy a surprise for him, to celebrate his promotion at work.

At the following session Nancy greeted me warmly: "I
feel better; the pressure is off. I do not feel so reluctant or
stuck; it's looser. I don't understand it but feel closer to it;
I see two sides and go back and forth." The decrease in
her anxiety seemed to make it easier for her to speak.

I found it useful to use Jung's vocabulary of ego and
Self. The ego side was coping with the illness and all its
accumulating duties of medical treatment, and especially
with the terror and rage at approaching death. The Self
side referred to what was pulling Nancy across the bound-
ary to what she called "A lovely, real place, a forgiving
place." We always asked of this place, What is this coming
toward me? Nancy said she felt air and energy circulating
between these two sides. Like the air of the dream it was
warm, supporting, alive. She said, "That is why people
want to be near me now," – meaning, despite her disfigu-
ration and all the grotesque aspects involved in her dying
– "they feel the air in the dream."

Nancy was facing death in *Pictures 6 and 7* (4/7/86)
done the same day. She said: "I do not know where they
came from. They came through me. I don't think I did

them." I asked if they came from the other side. "Yes," she said. "They show two sides. They are complete. It's not from me; it's just what is." I said, "Being." She agreed: "Yes exactly: real and peaceful; icons." In these paintings, Nancy said, the gold was the Self, and the purple the ego; again, the silver was the Self, the blue the ego.[62] She knew where she was, she said, and she had pictures to prove it.

Part III

Arriving

1. Necessary Images

We need images to approach death. Otherwise the vast silent dark overwhelms us.[63] Our religious tradition gives us the most startling image of all – resurrection. That which we love, which we value above all else, has been lost to us, and then is returned to us in a new form. The form, Scripture tells us, is so new that we, like the women at the tomb, do not recognize it at first (Mt: 28, Mk:16, Luke 24, John: 20). But the coming again of the one we love brings with it the power to recognize and receive it. The one we have lost, who is now present, is still the one we knew and loved. Resurrection of the body means life in a concrete and definite form that lives in continuity with the one we loved and lost.

Depth psychology tells us that we make our way to such startling images as the resurrection through the psyche. The reality of the image is not psychical but is mediated through the psyche. We must receive it, digest it, form images and myths of it, lay hold of it with all our heart and soul and mind and strength. Otherwise, it remains a mere idea without feet, a wish without guts, an ought without life; it lacks the flesh of concrete realization.

Religious tradition talks about the process of receiving God as corresponding with grace. Depth psychology talks about it as finding and creating our pattern, the motifs of imagery that form our special path. Out of chaos an order gradually emerges. This process is not unlike digestion; it stresses the fact that the soul is in the body. We take in all sorts of food and need moments of contemplation afterwards, to meditate upon what is given, to realize that it is given, and how it is shaped to be our own particular food, gathered into a pattern for receiving it and giving back into shared existence with others.[64] So it is with this psychic process in which the soul is in hiding. The soul is caught up in an internal sorting process, remaining in this life and yet open to the beyond. We keep something, get rid of something else, give this in love, give that in hate. This internal sorting process allows us a kind of living in the psyche which builds up space for our souls, an interiority that connects us with our daily world and all that is beyond it. It houses our core self.

Perhaps it was this soul space that Ruysbroeck saw named in secret by the "Sparkling Stone of God," Jesus Christ.[65] Winnicott describes the soul growth as "not only of body and of self in relation to objects [but] a growth going on inside, like a novel being all the time written, a world developing within the child."[66]

In making our myths about death, wrestling into images our experiences of the vast huge dark, we come face to face with the mystery that breaks all our pictures of death as we arrive at its borders. We arrive there to find its mystery coming to meet us from the other side. Then we see what our images have been – pointers to the arrival of the deepest dark there is, that is hidden in the light (like Picture 3), and of the brightest light that comes forward out of the dark.[67] Our images point to and prophesy the arrival of the one who comes to meet us from the other side.[68]

Nancy's wrestling with her illness and her encounter with that mystery that smashed her God-image were prophesies: they pointed to an impending arrival. She sensed a place that she was going to and that was coming to her that she called "forgiving." She said, "There is a part of it which is loving and kind, just kind; it doesn't want to hurt you. The hard part is the loss and the anger at the loss. It's very, very, hard – and I can do it." (4/17/86)

Nancy said those words in April after she had come to accept her death and felt a burst of happiness. I had the feeling that her anxiety had greatly decreased because she was making this catastrophe her own, accumulating its impact in the form of images, her own possessions, parts of her inner world that she gave back to the rest of us through her pictures. I often stressed with her how important her drawings were to us. But surely she knew that. She was setting out to explore a territory we had only heard of; we were depending on her to help us know about it. She, in turn, would say she could not be there looking into the dark if I was not there with her to know about it. We agreed that part of her transference to me now was my function as a "cattle prod."

Nancy got a jolt in May when one of her crucial tests indicated that the tumor was getting smaller. The news stirred the whole thing up again: it was as if she were getting all packed and ready to go and then the trip was canceled, or at least postponed. She wanted badly to be better but was scared to hope this might really happen, because, as she said, "I just don't see how it cannot be true that this will kill me; there is just a part of me that knows I am going to die from it.... I'm not well and that's that and I have to come to an understanding of it. But it's hard. I have to accept I may have more time than I thought, but I

don't have lots of time. I want to, but I don't. I mind that."
I said that perhaps the point is to build a bigger space,
tacking back and forth between the ego's reactions of
distress, confusion, hope, and anger, on one side, and the
Self on the other side that looks at the illness from a very
different point of view. Nancy took this in and dealt with
it. All her remaining pictures can be seen as wrestling with
opposites, encountering now one side, now the other,
and finally arriving at a union of both.

Picture 8 (5/6/86) came from her concentrated looking into the dark. She said of the figures on the left, "They
are on the other side; they're good and they're bad. They
are not as hostile as I thought they would be." Of the
square on the right, Nancy said, "The black is death, and
the lime green is the other side. It made me feel very
very frightened at first, but now it makes me feel very good,
very grounded." Months later, I came across a description
of a similar drawing in a book, *On Dreams and Death,* by
Marie-Louise von Franz: "The Hopi Indians of North Amer-
ica believe that the soul of the deceased goes through a
small square cavity, the so-called Sipàpu, which leads to
the Kiwa buildings. The cavity has the connotation of a
sacred place and is regarded as the place of origin, that
opening through which the Hopi tribe came up from the
depths to the surface of the world."[69] Of the circle, she
says, "The circle is an image of the Self ... colored and full
of life ... coming close to the Self there emanates from it
an attraction to it, and at the same time, a fear of it. The
fear of death is thereby in the last analysis a fear of the Self
and of the final inner confrontation with the Self."[70]

Picture 9 (5/15/86) focuses on the darkness. Nancy
said, "I don't want it to be like that, but that's what it's like
... I'm trying to find the right feeling. It's very dark when
you see the darkness. It's not simple; it's harder than you
think. I can't describe it because it is not, simple.... I want

to be able to see what it is because I want at least for you to understand it; it's so black." She had drawn the two figures on the left. Now right there, in the session, Nancy urgently drew the third, on the right. It is more human in shape. I need to say that Nancy had not only lost the ability to write or sign her name but also the use of her right hand was now failing too. It gave out as she drew, and she immediately switched to her left to draw this third figure, so intense was her need to picture it. She said of these presences, and of a fourth yet to appear, "They are like figures coming or waiting. It doesn't matter whether they are plus or minus; they are just there. It's very frightening; it's got a sense of purpose to it that's trying to put itself together and tell you about it. But it is cold, this dead cold, definitely a threat. But one part of me doesn't mind and one part of me hates it. It's got to be done and just go through it."

I was struck that just as Nancy struggled to find and create the right image for what was happening to her on her side, these figures seemed to be putting themselves together to appear from the other side.

Nancy felt thrown about by violent feelings and a desperation to see me. In one session (6/12/86), she spoke in brief halting phrases that punctuated her restless silences: "I hate doing this.... It's too wrong.... It's too far – " "To go?" I asked. "Yeah," she answered, "too far to go," meaning it was too far to go to die; meaning, dying was taking too long. Later she said, "I don't know what to make of it." When I asked if it were possible to say, "It is not right," and beyond that, "I don't know what to make of it, and yet I consent to it; I'll go with it," she answered, after groping a moment for words. "Yes it is. I like that, and it's fair."

But then the next week (6/19/86) she was very upset, and weeping. "Hard, hard," were the words that escaped

her constricting silences. "I don't want to be gone." The
worst for her was her speech coming and going, her
increasingly vanishing speech. "It drives me crazy. You
see, you can't get the right word! I'm losing it." I said,
"Even if you lose your speech, the center is intact." She
said then, "I just have to look at you." And then later, "I
could just kill, not being able to speak."

The following session (6/26/86) Nancy looked good
and greeted me with a clear sentence: "I just have to
touch you and hold your hand." She felt good and said
with confidence, "I do what I have to and it works, and if it
doesn't, that's OK." I say, "You are doing the work of
going back and forth across the gap, and soon you can
coast home." She said "That's all I need to know; it's a
relief." On that day, she was wearing the black-humor tee
shirt, green and purple and emblazoned with the words:
"THIS AIN'T NO WIENIE ROAST." She had planned to
have her husband roast hot dogs in the fireplace for
supper. She summed up: "It's hard, but it's also funny."

Nancy drew *Pictures 10, 11, 12, 13* (6/17/86, 6/20/86,
6/29/86, 6/30/86) just before and just after the last session, following upon her feelings of fright. These are
images full of color and life, much like those of the
colorful Self described by von Franz. Nancy made no
verbal comments about these pictures. Clearly, however,
she enjoyed them. They stand at opposite ends to the
earlier, fear-filled pictures. Those expressed dread. These
four brought out her sense of joy, even an airy freedom.
In sequence, Nancy was drawing her two sets of reactions
to what faced her: first dread, then positive expectation. It
is equally true to say that Nancy was drawing the contradictory aspects of what was coming towards her. These
four show the positive. The next to come depict anguish
and threat.

The first of these four (Picture 10), exhibits intense and varied color, firm brushstrokes, and alongside them, soft lines in pastel chalks. The purple, flowerlike form on the upper left is matched by fiery red lines boiling up from below in the center, banked by layers of turquoise, green, yellow, grey, brown, a deep blue, then green and gold on the right. All these strong forms and colors are balanced by a contrasting golden brown on the left, under the purple flower. We seem to be looking at an underwater world. It is a crowded scene, suggesting how packed with reactions Nancy was at the time, almost borne under by all her strong, condensed emotions. But the feeling is not negative – just full.

The other three pictures share an airy lightness, achieved by Nancy's use of so much unfilled white paper. The designs seem to float. Nancy managed some words to describe Picture 11: "Sun, Earth, Oceans, Eternal." Picture 12 even reveals some gaiety in the luminous orange-gold figure dancing toward the brilliant yellow one at the center. Their exact place, suspended over a ripple of black beneath them, reminds us that Nancy is not indulging in any denial of her serious situation. There is further feeling in the little purple figure to the right that resembles a bird taking wing. The sensation it conveys of soaring is fully developed in Picture 13, which Nancy drew the next day. Here four groups of birds – silver, gold, purple and yellow – all take flight into a sky just indicated by a dab of Robin's-egg blue on the left.

2. Ego-Self Paradox

The frightening black figures turned up again and again in all the subsequent drawings, right up until Nancy stopped painting in mid-October, when she could no longer sit up or coordinate her movements. Her painting had undergone astonishing changes. Color was added in abundance to the frightening black figures; then later, lines began to appear in them, as if to define their essence. Moreover, positive and negative figures appeared in the same pictures. Then the negative and positive appeared in the same single figure.

Picture 14 (7/3/86) shows a luminous yellow and red figure in profile holding its hand out to two figures, one purple, one brown. The placement of these figures, in intimate relation, the yellow and red one addressing the other two, imparts a sense of something important and positive being said. The effect is both calming and stirring.

Picture 15 (7/8/86) shows the jagged figures in the background over which defining lines are superimposed. These are the figures Nancy saw waiting for her.

In *Picture 16* (7/15/86) the figures take shape. The black jagged lines along the left side and top express anxiety, anger, terror. These are the waiting figures. Note the torn nature of the paper, especially the left side, expressing perhaps the way Nancy felt about her life, just torn apart, leaving her mere scraps. Yet she was also plunged into strong immediate experience. She did not plan or plot these paintings, nor execute them with slow precision. She was just gazing into the dark and trying to capture quickly what she saw.[71]

Picture 17 (7/24/86) presents four figures again, all in black, with a jagged black line clearly expressing agitation, perhaps even fury, at the bottom. All the figures are precisely defined presences.

Picture 18 (7/25/86) brings into play the same kind of figures, now all in color. The jagged black lines in the left corner have softened to grey. We can see in this sequence how Nancy moved back and forth across the gap facing her, as if weaving connections, first from one side, then from the other. She tried to talk to me about the drawings but could not form the words. She would shrug, smile and then suddenly blurt out, "Everything and nothing! Joy and sadness! Full and not-full! Home and not-home!"

Nancy was never entirely released from the terror and outrage she felt about her illness and the threat of impending death that accompanied it. That side of the gap and the awful fear that the gap was nothing but an abyss waiting to swallow her up stayed with her until the end. The other side of the gap grew stronger and stronger; we will see in the later drawings that the color from this side came to contain the black.

Picture 19 (7/27/86) shows the group of mysterious figures expanded to six. Four of them appear with muted grey backgrounds, two with embracing mauve lines, two moving toward warm green lines. The remaining two figures are bright gold with touches of aqua within them. The darkest of the figures, at the center, gestures toward its right, if we view the figures as facing us, just touching the figure next to it there. What we have here is a variety of presences or perhaps, we might say, presence presenting itself in a variety of ways. The effect is warm and touching, to convey something Nancy could no longer say in words. At best, ejaculatory words would burst from her.

In *Picture 20* (7/29/86), the dreaded dark figures soften, like the jagged lines in Picture 18, to grey, and beyond that, at the center, to a warm blue, and they all surmount the dramatic white of the bottom half of the page. Defining lines in the dark reach out in a pronounced gold, the color Nancy identified as the Self in her earliest icon (Picture 6). Nancy made good use of Jung's vocabulary of ego and Self to describe her spiritual journey. I was impressed by the way that vocabulary helped her navigate the vast distances and gave her words and images to convey the great gap she experienced between her different reactions to her dying. The contrast was great and she knew it, and one way or another she told us about it.

To her ego, her death-dealing illness always appeared as a catastrophe; in the part of her ego related to Self, she saw the illness as an essential part of her path. Her work during the spring, summer, and early fall months was to hold these two sets of opposing reactions together, denying neither one or the other, nor letting them split into mutually excluding perceptions. This was strenuous work indeed. Nancy was tempted, and I was, too, to yield to the ancient reductive interpretation: life is hard; life gets harder; and then you die. We were also tempted in an opposite direction, to side only with the prospective interpretation that everything she suffered revealed some substantial meaning and therefore was not, just all right, but redeeming.

Neither interpretation would do by itself. Many times Nancy found herself stuck in a place between these opposites, without solution or resolution.

We must remember the successive breakings of the frame of her work. First, the frame of her analysis broke when the regularity of her sessions was disrupted by the strain of coping with her illness. Nancy wrestled successfully to find a new container. The analysis reframed itself, around the task of how to approach death. Then the frame of discourse broke again when the tumor stole language and speech from her and her use of her dreams as links to the transcendent. Her God-image and all that mediated the beyond to her were smashed. But then Nancy found a new and intensely feminine way of communicating, through empathy and identification, a being-in-the-midst of the raging opposites that besieged her. She reframed the analysis through quick, deliberate experience of her own pictures. That created a psychic space large enough to include the starkly opposed worlds of living and dying. Now her pictures pointed to the arrival of something from the beyond that Nancy felt coming to meet her and that she knew she was going toward. Whatever this arriving presence was, it broke the frame of analysis. It was bigger and darker than any of our anticipations or preconceptions. And it did not arrive ready-made or in anything like a clear form. It seemed instead to gather itself into shape in response to Nancy's efforts to deal with it.

In *Picture 21* (8/5/86), the waiting figures and the lines that define them are all in color. The black border has become blue and the fifth figure on the right blends into that border.

In *Picture 22* (8/18/86), we again see five figures with no dark border at all but with what has become a familiar torn-off edge to the paper at the right. The strong black figure at the center is contained, held in place, by colored figures. The silver one next to the black reaches out to it. Silver, we might remember from the earlier icon, Picture 7, represents the Self. In this picture, the ego's worst fears are confirmed and surrounded, and the Self figure reaches out to establish connection to them.

Slowly navigating back and forth across the gap, Nancy found her way. Jung describes such a voyage to the depths: "If all goes well, the solution, seemingly of its own accord, appears.... Then and only then is it convincing. It is felt as grace. Since the solution proceeds out of the confrontation and clash of opposites, it is usually an unfathomable mixture of conscious and unconscious factors, and therefore a symbol, a coin split into two halves which fit together precisely." [72] In a footnote Jaffé adds, "One of the meanings of *symbolon* is the *tessera hospitalitatis* between host and guest, the broken coin which is shared between two parting friends." [73]

The dream image of coins that came to Nancy from the feminine spirit took on layers of meaning – connecting her dream-ego to her waking-ego, her living to her dying self, her two sets of reactions to death, her self to my self, and her dying self to her living self, the one that was to fall into the green and pleasant land.

Part of Nancy's solution was precisely the coins of passage of the cliff dream, a bequest of the spirit of the feminine. I believe she received those coins of passage through her work in the feminine mode with her drawings. Her struggle to depict her experience of dying and somehow communicate it to me enabled her to go back and forth across the gap of opposites until it transformed itself into a space of imaginative living and dying. Here she was, a gentle graceful woman, swollen and misshapen from steroids and radiation, exercising an unflinching capacity to look into what faced her in the dark and then persevering until she could draw it. She set to work every morning after breakfast, sitting at her table, and later in bed, with paper, crayon, and paint. Her drawings expressed both her terror and her joyous feeling at being able to capture in images her sense that she was going somewhere. Her drawings were prophesies. From a psychological point of view, we can describe Nancy's work as building up the transcendent function in her.[74] We see in her drawings her own ego point of view – with its plans and hopes, frustrations and fears, confronted by another presence that looks at what is happening entirely differently."[75] This can be called the Self, the center of the whole psyche, conscious and unconscious. But in this other side, something beyond the psyche rises up, something that transcends the whole psyche.

We are given three meanings of transcendent here: The first refers to contents that transcend ego consciousness and come from the unconscious. The second is what is properly called a function, through which we build up the capacity to hear both viewpoints, the ego's and that of the unconscious contents that challenge the ego's hopes. The ego's effort to enter into the conversations between these conflicting opposites transforms the gap between them into a space large enough to embrace both perspectives. Gradually, the listening across the enlarged gap yields a sense of a beyond that directly concerns itself with our struggle. Indeed, it seemed to Nancy that not only was she going some place "kind and forgiving"' but that it was offering itself to her. This is the third meaning of transcendent: a force that comes from beyond the whole psyche.

From a religious point of view, we can see this work Nancy was doing as readying her to correspond with grace, to receive what was offered her. She did not deny what was happening to her but opened herself to all – good and bad. From a psychological point of view, this shuttling function, going back and forth from ego to Self, moves toward a solution that transcends both. We could describe it as building up an ego-related-to-Self, or might use the alchemical notion of constructing a "subtle body," which is not unlike what Christians call the glorified, or mystical, or resurrected body.[76]

Here we live in paradox, between and within the opposites of "what I want" and "what it wants." In Christian terms, the same paradox enunciates itself in prayer when we put forward what we want with as much boldness and passion as we can muster while at the same time we open ourselves to the Other who lives both deep within and far outside us. Thus it is we pray, "Not my will but Thy will be done."

We can see all of this in *Picture 23* (8/27/86). Here six new kinds of figures appear. They are composed entirely of lines, each describing a similar shape. The largest stands

on the left. Thereafter, the figures descend in height
down to the smallest, on the right. The bright colors –
brown, gold, green, and red – belong to the four figures
within the line-up, held between a black figure on the left
and a grey one on the right. The framing of brightness
within dark, shaded colors suggests Nancy's struggle with
the suffering she felt in her swollen body and declining
energy and everything in her that exploded from her with
the word "Hard!" Yet an airiness persists in the lines set
against the white paper, and in the sense of perspective
hinted at, as if the figures were stepping forward from
some distance and at the same time leading the viewer's
eye toward their faraway place of origin. They give us a
sense of buoyancy – "home" is the word Nancy spoke
here.

Picture 24 (9/4/86) fills its paper with closely packed
water colors in light bright shades. The warm dense brown
on the right halts the progression of color across the page
from left to right, and undergirds it at the bottom of the
page as it moves in the opposite direction, from right to
left. The density of colors so compactly aligned conveys a
feeling of weight, of elements pressing in upon each other. But still the smudging of the brown against the clear
white paper, worked onto the familiar torn-off right mar-
gin, provides a positive perspective. Seen from this van-
tage-point, the brown, violet, and red colors stand before
the yellow, green, and orange stripes, as if stepping forward either to greet or to threaten, while the yellow,
green, and orange receive us comfortably into their wel-
coming background. The blue stripe on the far left is
pleasingly ambiguous, stepping in front of the orange
and yet somehow reaching behind it at the same time.
This is the changing landscape of Nancy's everyday life.

Picture 25 (9/8/86) presents opposites again. The one
solid black negative figure on the far right is outweighed

by three boldly positive ones. A shining yellow figure, with brown lines inside it, stands assured in its strength on the left, next to a silver figure crossed with gold lines which precedes a vivid orange one with green lines. These three, in vivid colors with inner lines that suggest a lively interior life, do not deny the grave signified by the all-black figure but are not conquered by it. The black seems softer now, its darkness divided, diluted, more friendly.

Picture 26 (9/9/86) presents us with the drama of four standing figures, the totality of the human, with blackness to express terror and at the bottom and up the left side jagged lines shouting anger. In the midst stands a fifth figure of silver, very much like the Self of the early icon (Picture 7). The black figure nearest the left side reaches to and indeed actually touches the silver. In the body of this silver presence we can glimpse defining lines of gold, indicating perhaps a still greater contrast with the mournful black. The gold represents a transcendence within the transcendent, pointing to something from the beyond drawing near to us.

Picture 27 (9/23/86) retains the lines and bright colors, but with two unmistakable changes which persist until the very end. There are no defined figures now and no black at all. A sea-green color suggests the presence of just two figures, though pink, gold, and blue lines within the green point to a possible three. The blue holds lines of gold within itself, a gold just hinted at in the smear of intense red on the far left. The interplay of lines with overlapping colors suggests that a precise location of presence is not to be given, just felt. The whole picture gives a promise of warmth, of beauty.

The promise seems fulfilled in *Picture 28* (10/8/86), the last one that Nancy painted. Here only the essential lines remain, in a wash of color in the two right-hand figures and in a bright mixture of colors in the central figure. That which so slowly emerged throughout all the previous paintings now emerges and stands forth in an imagery of a transformed nature. What was merely glimpsed is finally sharply revealed. The black is gone. There appear to be strong pointers to a new encounter, perhaps an ultimate transformation.

3. Transformation

Nancy wrestled with strongly contending opposites in that time of gaps between life and death, and between ego and Self. She encountered the vast dark outside and beyond her God-image. She had arrived at that space of transformation where pointers to and from the beyond were prophesying what was coming to her. All – wrestlings, encounters, arrival – reverberated in the world around her. Her husband, her friends, her parents, her brothers were caught up in her struggles, and all emerged from them with something of great moment for themselves. I was drawn into the suffering of these people, too, as I came and went from my sessions with Nancy. Sometimes, at their request, I spoke with them about their feelings. I was able to break the boundaries that framed Nancy's analysis because we had held to them so firmly with our fixed weekly hour, always, no matter what, at the same time, and with our consistent focus on the task of living toward death.

Because transference and countertransference are pivotal in analytic process, a word is in order here, I think, about my own experience in sharing Nancy's journey. To work with someone who is dying brings something more than just some special inflections into one's life; one feels threat, danger, upsetting possibilities at every level of countertransference. The subjective levels of normal countertransference, as one person to another, are well enough known. We also understand that sort of abnormal countertransference where our own complexes may be drawn into response to an analysand, signalling that we have more work to do for ourselves. We work hard, then, to minimize the effect of our own problems on our analysands and our interpretations of their material. The objective level of countertransference – all that the person's unconscious life induces in our feeling life – offers us important clues to what an analysand may be experiencing.[77] We can learn from reactions stirred up in us that we know are alien to us that we are in fact feeling what the analysand feels, but not consciously. This new conduit of information creates a curious bond and a strong one between analyst and analysand.

Such countertransference experience was especially valuable after Nancy lost her use of words.. Then both of us had to rely upon empathy and identification with the other to communicate. Another perspective, what I would call a transcendent one, seemed to infuse our struggles with all the accountrements of illness – medical tubes, oxygen tanks, Nancy's bodily imbalance, her fallings off into feebleness, her blindness in one eye, her incontinence, and the constant emotional undertow of something verging on despair. The transcendent perspective insisted that we include all of this – the machines, the human wreckage, everything negative, along with the positive insights and the views ahead, all of the now and the beyond.

When an analysand's experience is of the advent of death, the analyst must deal with countertransference reactions on each of three levels. First, there is one's response to a particular suffering in a particular person. Second, there are any unworked-through problems or complexes around death and dying that may beset the analyst. Third, there are the clues to the analysand's experience of mortality, conveyed now in semi-conscious and unconscious and unvoiced reactions, in word, posture, gesture. Because Nancy finally lost her voice, this third level of transference and countertransference proved the most valuable of the three. The risks were great; we knew that. At any time either one of us could be pulled across the borders. And always we were faced with the urgent tasks of the here-and-now, of this place at this moment.

Jung catches the welter of reactions here and their complexity: "The presence of a person dying ... has a definite effect upon one's unconscious ... [it] makes the world unreal and strengthens the unconscious so that it often forms a vortex in which one is sucked under. Be careful that this does not happen to you: Try to touch things that remind you of your reality." [78] In the opposite direction, Jung reminds us, "... when a person with whom one was intimate dies, either one is oneself drawn into the death, so to speak, or else this burden has the opposite effect of a task that has to be fulfilled in real life.... A bit of life has passed over from the dead to the living and compels him towards its realization." [79]

These opposing psychological reactions are mirrored in the ambiguities of religious images of the beyond. They suggest but do not seem to want to define the life to come. They seem unrealistic and yet stir our hopes for life after death. Religious images here more than anywhere else must be hazy, multifaceted, contradictory, because in them we confront the infinite in terms of the finite. Their necessary ambiguity stirs up matching responses in us. We wonder, with such images of a life still to come, if we are just making it all up out of wishful longings or the denial of our fear of death. But then something breaks through to us that silences all our maunderings with its own formidable presence. There is comfort to be found, I think, in

Dorothy Emmet's words about the ambivalence of religious symbols as intrinsic to their nature, not as "the result of pious vagueness or confusion of thought.... It is a precise way of conveying the fundamental dilemma of religious symbolism, which presents the analogue of the transcendent in the forms of the phenomenal, of the infinite in the finite." [80]

Nancy was not my first experience of death as an analyst. Nor was she my first patient to die from a ravaging disease.[81] Nonetheless, her circumstances pulled on me as few others, because of the long work we had done together and continued to do up until the day before she died, and because of the person she was, her gentleness and toughness, her constant reaching for the center, whatever it might be, positive or negative, friendly or unfriendly. I felt myself pulled into her suffering, registering it not only consciously but in dream reactions.[82] I felt exhausted from all the strenuous work seeing her in hospital or home, up, down, clear, uncertain. I felt sad, disheartened; so much of her life was just coming and going to the hospital, tests, operations. But there was more: periodically, I registered the certainty growing in me that each of us – Nancy, me, everyone – must live his or her life to the fullest each day and could find the resources to do so.

There were delicate technical issues of how to keep the work within an analytical frame while I was being drawn into meeting and trying to help family members, friends, and nurses. The issues sorted themselves out as the focus of our work really ceased to be upon personal problems. They were gone.

The incidents of her daily life Nancy took up with her husband, and gladly. There was nothing now they could not talk about. Our sessions concerned themselves almost exclusively with the fact of dying and Nancy's moving back and forth between ego-reactions and Self-reactions to that central fact. She met what she saw – and what was now asked of her – with grit, anger, a sense of great loss, whatever was called out in her. After her death, I learned from her husband that from the time of her acceptance of the fact that she was dying, in late March and April, Nancy seldom spoke of it. All that went into the analytical work.

Another great concern rose in me when Nancy began to fade, in the last months before her death. Should I charge her for sessions in which I was not doing the usual analytic work? I had already come to terms with keeping the fee in place when we had full-length sessions, and not charging for briefer visits I made to the hospital or travel time to and from her house, even if it took up most of a morning, as it usually did. And certainly I would not increase her fee when in the time of her illness I raised my fees generally. But should I go on charging her at all? I finally decided I would do so, because we were doing analytical work; that was the reason I was there, not as friend or priest or family member, but as analyst. Although our means were unorthodox, our task was the appointed one, the trustworthy one of analytical work – what does consciousness say, what does the unconscious say, what do the drawings tell us, what do the transference-countertransference affects tell us? It felt wrong to me to break the container in any way.

Before her illness, as I mentioned earlier, Nancy pictured me in her transference as her cheerleader, which was her way of saying she experienced my empathic mirroring of her as a woman as well as an analysand. In her illness she relied on my continuing presence, saying frequently that she could not face the dark of dread if I were not there to know and to want to know about it. She felt through me a link with the world, felt she was contributing to our knowledge of life on the other side. She thought of me as a constant prod to make her do the work of consenting to her own reactions and communicating them in drawings. She talked at first about writing something about her experiences. When she no longer could hold a pen, she asked me to do so and agreed to have me do so. She made of me the missing feminine nurturing voice, something linked to the spirit in her dream that gave her the coins of passage. Sometimes she responded to me on a much lustier instinctual level, such as that greeting when we renewed contact in September, after a month's recess: "Oh, I could just eat you!"

Nancy used me to help her hear her feelings, especially the sadness and depression whose undertow always exerted a pull on her to withdraw altogether. She had a place in her sessions to vent her rage and terror and to find some way of sorting through them. Her nurses told me that after I left, at the end of a session, Nancy would fall into a deep restful sleep. It was part of that structuring of her day that began with painting as the first of the ways she could explore what was happening to her. Then she was free just to be the rest of the day. At our sessions she would show me her paintings and struggle to speak about what they depicted. The rest of the week she would leave the darker experiences alone; she had her appointed time for them.

I felt drawn into the play and great collision of opposites. I could not help feeling an animal revulsion at the nearness of death, with all that machinery, the smells, the grotesque deformations of skin and body. And yet I had to acknowledge to myself that I felt pulled right past all that to the person of Nancy who was always there, unmistakably alive in her dying.

Her ability to go on being the person she was had a great deal to do with her husband's attentions. He always treated her as if she was fully there, participating in her life, to be consulted about everything, even the gravesite. One of the reasons he decided to go to medical school, in his mid-forties, to become an oncologist, was to show people how much could be done for the quality of living and dying if we remembered in cases like this one that this is a person who had a tumor – not a tumor that possessed a person.

Nancy was deeply grateful for her husband's help, often saying she could not get through her suffering without him. She was well aware of her privileged position, being able to die at home in their bedroom, surrounded by flowers, with all her pictures on the wall, in a bed with fresh linen sheets. We talked sometimes of the plight of most people, left to die in the impersonal surroundings of hospitals and nursing homes. Her experience underlines Kohut's point about our human need for selfobjects[83] all our life long, as well as Simone Weil's defining question: The only question to ask our neighbor, Weil said, is, "What are you going through?"[84] That recognizes the precious "you" in people. And so, in her version of Kohut and Weil, Nancy acted to support her husband in his grief. She asked me to tell him her ski dream because of the comfort he might find in it. She schemed to surprise him with a gift when he got his promotion and award. And she insisted he go off for three weeks in the summer to a course vital to his scientific work.

I found my own speechlessness in Nancy's plight, the plight of all of us in meeting death. Wonderful as her care was, it was not enough to stay the wound of unlived life, the pain and disfigurement inching their way along with their killing touch. What made some words come was the clear demonstration of Nancy trying so valiantly to live her dying. Forced to that place "at the still point of the turning world," she was looking around to see what she could see.[85] I was excited to hear from her what she was seeing and feeling. She taught me. I saw what was there and not there. We ventured. We found words together. Often I came away knowing we had reached a new frontier.

In Melanie Klein's terms, the work of reparation was going on – our anger, sadness, and aggression were being matched and transformed by spontaneous reparative moments – Nancy and I bursting into laughter at the awfulness of life, or another time, over a remark she made about her husband, which I told him after Nancy was dead, when he asked me if she had ever mentioned him.[86] Nancy had said, when I asked how things were going with her husband, "He's useless. But I think I'll keep him." He laughed long and hard.

I felt useless, too, often enough. Was I fooling myself, feeling and thinking that we were still doing serious analytic work? Was I just being wishful or sentimental? For Nancy was dying, and nothing would stop that. But then I realized that a feeling of uselessness rose from the premise that material reality was all there is to reality. What in fact made a decisive difference to the quality of this experience and gave it its unmistakable richness was the analytical framework, with all its limits. It pointed sharply, persuasively beyond itself. What was reparative for Nancy was in some way the same for me.

Even when damage was incurred by my other patients – and there was one instance when I made a bad mistake – reparation was the final effect. One day I saw a woman right after seeing Nancy; I was overloaded with death and dying. This woman had cast me in her transference as a good-mother figure she needed to protect her fragile ego against the destructive force of bad-mother emotions. Now, as a result of my carrying death issues with me into the consulting room, she saw me as the bad-mother incarnate, and she risked all the rage and attack she never dared experience before against her mother and the re-

lated parts of herself. She had somatized them and suffered years of physical distress as a result.

My carelessness in this instance, as I moved from analysand to analysand, taught me I needed a buffer zone
between my times with Nancy and the beginning of my
day's work. I could not depend on so useful an outburst as
the second patient had provided. I needed space and
time after sessions with Nancy. This I provided for myself
by walking the mile and a half from Nancy's apartment,
through Central Park, to my office. This walk came to be a
period of mindlessness and of meditation. I let what happened go into me and through me and find its own roots.
This added a tougher perspective to my work with all my
different people. I brought directly into our work the
awareness we all possess but pay scant attention to – that
we do not live forever, that we must receive and take the
life offered us with a gusto and gratitude we usually do
not dare.

In sum, then, like Nancy, I was hurled back and forth
between opposites and forced to build up the transcendent function in myself by a constant motion between my
own ego-reactions of sadness, horror, compassion, anger,
depression, and reactions from the Self side that evoked
discovery, new insights, a sense of being gathered up into
the arrival of the meaning of central religious truths, such
as resurrection.

My small experience mirrored Nancy's large one of
transforming the gap between living and dying, between
ego and Self, into a creative space for living richly right up
to the end. Nancy effected this transformation through
her pictures, which were at once inner events and outer
representations. We effected the transformation through
a deliberate use of the feminine mode of being, which
changed the gap of wordlessness into the speech of mutual exchange. The sharply defined boundaries, between

self and other, between personal and collective layers of the psyche, were breaking down. We were living now in a third area some of the time, where creativity did not exclude violent aggressive feelings. We worked in a confrontational area structured by images – the letting go of the cliff, the coins of passage, the green land to which the moist holding air conducted her, images of dark figures, of jagged fury, images of lines of light that shot through the dark. Slowly we stitched meaning together, making the unbearable bearable, supporting the unsupportable.

One day after seeing Nancy, when I was walking back to my office across the park, I felt in the grey wet weather and lowering clouds and general winter bleakness a mirroring of the horror of what she had endured. Suddenly, I was startled by the sound of a neighing of horses. I looked across a big field to where two dark horses stood pawing and prancing under their police riders. Nancy's early picture of a giant black horse's hoof came to me, stepping down from the sky to squash everything beneath it (Picture 2) – lethal in its way like the Wizards' voices. Then, swiftly, the two horses and riders broke into a jubilant rush across the field in front of me, racing to see who would first reach the other side. Arriving, the horses stamped around, snorting, lashing their tails, their riders laughing with pleasure. Before I knew it, they were off again in the opposite direction, traversing the field with boundless energy. Was this, I thought, Nancy's old repressed energy getting free, ready now to gallop to the other side? It filled me with unspeakable joy.

Such synchronistic events turned up more than once, affording glimpses of a large unity that reconciles all the jagged edges of our hurtful lives.[87] I saw new facts about this "other life" and I saw, with shock, that a feminine mode of being was needed to see and understand them. We need this mode to enter the gap and to do the work that will transform it into a creative space of aliveness. That space-in-between meets the dark side of God, meets the God outside our experiences of the divine caught up in our God-images.

Such events are annunciations. Our responses need some of Mary's graceful response. Both the events and our responses point to our utter dependence upon and interdependence with each other. I saw the truth of Nancy saying she could not be in the dark without my being there to know about it, and the fact that I could not meditate on the ends of life without her experiences before me. We not only need each other, all this insisted. We cannot exist without each other. So the "soul friends" that select themselves, on the basis of each person's connections to the Self, offer us glimpses of the great community that is born in this space of creative living and dying, and that seems to survive after death.

Nancy arrived at a sense of communion based not on proximity nor expediency but on persons one by one connecting to the center. This sense of communion generates community. We share an intangible but palpable presence in being, however little we talk about it. We depend on each other to reach this. It is also what makes us so impatient with the kind of false collectivity that pretends to be community – a sameness that is coerced, a forced altruism that amounts to little more than bullying and complying.

4. Arrival

There came a time in the late fall when Nancy's work of bringing ego and Self together was finished. She was fearfully ill and could barely make a sound. She had gone as far as she could with bringing and holding the opposing forms of life and death together in her dying days. Now it was time to rest in the dark and coast home. Sometimes she sat propped up in bed, sometimes lay flat, holding my hand, looking at me, uttering a few words about how hard it was, or just looking. Gradually she became absolutely silent, though clearly present and alert. I began to read to her, passages from her Jung books that she had especially liked. At the end of the sessions now I would read her a psalm. She would slip off into sleep, and as she did, I would sit and hum or sing to her.

By the second part of January, it was clear the end was coming soon. One day, thinking about Nancy, an idea arrived with the utter conviction of its rightness: It was to read aloud to her the notes of her analysis from the time of the beginning of her illness, a little more than a year's sessions. It was a kind of ritual of separation and arrival.

Nancy was flat on her back now, unable to open her eyes much, but I could feel her intense listening. Her eyelids would flutter, and occasionally she would open them and look at me, or her thumb would brush against my fingers. In the last weeks, I read through all our sessions of her months of illness. The notes summarized her preparation for dying and the understanding she was gathering and gladly receiving. She would sleep deeply after each session, her nurse told me.

I finished the reading the day before she died. I ended with a psalm and that lovely prayer of Cardinal Newman's:

> May God support us all the day long, until the shadows lengthen and the evening comes, and the busy world is hushed, and the fever of life is over, and our work is done. Then in thy mercy grant us a safe lodging and a holy rest and peace at the last.

Nancy died early the next morning.

Nancy had no formal religious faith, yet she possessed a religious sensibility. She made use of Jung's vocabulary of ego and Self as a kind of makeshift theological language – and it worked. Jung's vocabulary provided direction, helped her navigate the distances between her first experience of the illness as catastrophe and her later conviction that this terrible tumor was in fact an integral and necessary part of her life. Her illness was part of her way, leading her to ultimate arrival where she belonged. Her work in this last year of analysis was to hold these two sets of opposing reactions together, neither denying one nor the other, not letting them split her apart.

Nancy wrestled with her divine messenger and messages and, like Jacob, felt herself both wounded and blessed in the encounter. Out of her wrestling came images that made clear what struggle was like in her remarkable sequence of paintings. We see in them how she moved from staring with dread into the dark to looking through the dark to a light within and beyond it. She developed that extraordinary capacity to look into the gap between darkness and light, life and death, from the ego side with its outrage and despair, and from the Self with its abundant permissiveness and majestic promise.

Nancy arrived at a transformation of the gap into a space of prophecy, pointing to what was coming to her. It was a "lovely," "kind," and "forgiving place" she saw ahead of her; we cannot forget that. It was a place, she understood, that did not seek to hurt anyone. She expressed it symbolically in her "icon" paintings, Pictures 6 and 7. "Both sides exist," this iconography proclaims. The sides touch each other; together they form an unmistakable and pleasing whole. Nancy did not know where they came from, or exactly where they led, even though she had painted them. It was enough to call them, as we did, "windows onto eternity."

Notes

1. Ann Belford Ulanov, "Picturing God," in *Picturing God* (Cambridge: Cowley, 1986).
2. See Ann Belford Ulanov, *The Female Ancestors of Christ* (Boston: Shambhala, 1993).
3. Jung writes that the soul "has the dignity of an entity endowed with, and conscious of, a relationship to deity." ... "I did not attribute a religious function to the soul, I merely produced the facts which prove the soul is *naturaliter religiosa*, i.e., possesses a religious function." C.G. Jung, *Psychology and Alchemy, Collected Works,* Vol. 12, trans. R.F.C. Hull (New York: Pantheon, 1958), pp. 10, 13; para. 11, 14.

   Jung deepens his point: "The tremendous effectiveness (mana) of these images is such that they not only give one the feeling of pointing to the *Ens realissimum*, but make one convinced that they actually express it and establish it as a fact. ... It is, in fact, impossible to demonstrate God's reality to oneself except by using images which have arisen spontaneously or are sanctified by tradition, and whose psychic nature and effects the naive-minded person has never separated from their unknowable metaphysical background. He instantly equates the effective image with the transcendental *X* to which it points. ... It must be remembered that the image and the statement are psychic processes which are different from their transcendental object; they do not posit it, they merely point to it." C.G. Jung, *Answer to Job,* in *Psychology and Religion: West and East, Collected Works,* Vol. 11, trans. R.F.C. Hull (New York: Pantheon, 1958), p. 363, para. 558.

   For discussion of Jung's distinction among depth psychologists because of his interest in the infinite, see Ann Belford

Ulanov, "A Shared Space," *Quadrant* (New York: C.G. Jung Foundation, Spring 1985).

4. Ann Belford Ulanov, *The Wisdom of the Psyche* (Cambridge: Cowley, 1987), pp. 18ff. A God-image may turn out to be something unexpected, even negative, like a drinking problem or an addiction, or a chronic inferiority complex. Such a problem can function like a god in that the whole personality revolves around it and is united, even under its negative influence.

5. Ann and Barry Ulanov, *Cinderella and Her Sisters: The Envied and the Envying* (Louisville: Westminster, 1983), Chapter 13.

6. C.G. Jung *Letters*, 2 vols., eds. Gerhard Adler and Aniela Jaffé, trans. R.F.C. Hull (Princeton: Princeton University Press, 1973), I, p. 40, 5.26.23.

7. Marie-Louise von Franz, *Alchemy, An Introduction to the Symbolism and Psychology* (Toronto: Inner City Books, 1959), p. 139.

8. I present this material with Nancy's permission to do so and with gratitude to her for allowing me to do so.

9. See Julian of Norwich, *The Revelations of Divine Love*, trans. James Walsh, S.J. (New York: Harper & Brothers, 1961), p. 7; see also, *Complete Works of St. Teresa*, 3 vols., trans. and ed. E. Allison Peers (London: Sheed and Ward, 1957), Vol. 1, p. 24.

10. C.G. Jung, "The Secret of the Golden Flower," in *Alchemical Studies*, *CW* 13, trans. R.F.C. Hull (Princeton: Princeton University Press, 1967), p. 48, para. 41.

11. C.G. Jung "The Stages of Life," in *CW* 8, *The Structure of the Psyche*, trans. R.F.C. Hull (New York: Pantheon, 1960), p. 395, para. 773.

12. See Marion Milner, "The Framed Gap," 1952 in *The Suppressed Madness of Sane Men* (London: Tavistock, 1987), pp. 80-81.

13. Aniela Jaffé, "Interview," *Psychological Perspectives*, Spring-Summer, 1988, p. 91.

14. See Michael Eigen, "Breaking the Frame: Stopping the World," *Modern Psychoanalysis*, Vol. VI, No. 1, 1981, p. 96. See also Ann Belford Ulanov, "Needs, Wishes, and Tran-

scendence," in *Picturing God.* Controversy has flared over how tight this frame of analysis should be. At one extreme clinicians who advocate a tight frame, emphasizing strict adherence to method and deemphasizing the personal relationship of analyst and analysand, are accused of narcissistic and rigid personalities reducing the whole of a person's world to an hour with an analyst. Further, it is speculated that such tightness orders an inner chaos in which analysts must flounder. At the opposite extreme, those who advocate a loose frame are accused of trespassing the boundaries of the analytical container, blurring or breaking them altogether. They are compelled to do so, this reasoning goes, because of inner rigidities that threaten to dry them up.

For myself I think these divisions can be important or nothing at all, a pseudo-issue. We cannot divorce the method from the work. Yet the work is not the method alone. Jung is useful here: "In reality, everything depends on the man and little or nothing on the method. The method is really the path, the direction taken by a man; the way he acts is the true expression of his nature. If it ceases to be this, the method is nothing more than an affectation, something artificially pieced on, rootless and sapless ... a means of fooling oneself and evading what may perhaps be the implacable law of one's being...." "The Secret of the Golden Flower," *CW* 13, p. 7, para. 4.

15. M. Heidegger, *Being and Time,* trans. J. Macquarrie and E. S. Robinson (New York: Harper, 1962), p. 174.

16. See "H.D.: Tribute to Freud," in Nor Hall, *Those Women* (Dallas: Spring, 1988); see also Peter Gay, *Freud, A Life for Our Time* (New York: Anchor Doubleday, 1988), p. 303 where Gay describes Freud remitting patients' fees when they fell on hard times, making friends of his favorite patients, conducting an informal analysis of his colleague Eitington during evening strolls in Vienna. See also P. Roazen, *Freud and His Followers* (New York: Knopf, 1975), Chapter IX. See also Esther Menaker, *Appointment in Vienna* (New York: St. Martin's Press, 1988), p 95: "They forgot that Freud himself reacted in 'forbidden' ways to his patients' needs; some-

times he fed them, sometimes advised them in matters regarding important life decisions, sometimes helped them financially or aided them in finding employment." See also S. Freud, "Recommendations to Physicians Practicing Analysis," in *Standard Edition*, Vol. XII, trans. James Strachey (London: Hogarth, 1973), pp. 115, 118. See also Margaret Little, "Winnicott Working in Areas Where Psychotic Anxieties Predominate," in *Psychotic Anxieties and Containment* (New York: Jason Aronson, 1990). See also Masud Khan, *When Spring Comes, Awakenings in Clinical Psychoanalysis* (London: Chatto & Windus, 1988), pp. 96-97, 111, 195, 198-201.

17. Jung, *Letters*, I, p. 456, 4/21/47.

18. Nancy found encouragement for her drawings from a class she took from Dr. Edith Wallace at the C.G. Jung Foundation, New York City.

19. See R.D. Laing, *The Politics of Experience* (New York: Pantheon, 1967), Chapter 3.

20. For examples of negative animus problems, see Ann Belford Ulanov, *The Feminine in Jungian Psychology and in Christian Theology* (Evanston: Northwestern University Press, 1971), pp. 246, 254, 260, 262-268, 317.

21. We can ask about the meaning of the "accident" to Nancy's leg. From the ego point of view, that of rationality and commonsense, of course accidents do happen. But from the point of view of the whole psyche, of the conscious and unconscious, such an accident to her leg might be seen as the Self telling Nancy to wake up; she had been living from the wrong standpoint. Nancy herself felt that.

22. *The Herder Symbol Dictionary*, trans. Boris Matthews (Wilmette: Chiron, 1986), p. 180.

23. Jung, *Letters*, Vol. I, p. 509, 9/30,/48.

24. *Ibid.*, p. 517, 1/8/49.

25. See Russell A. Lockhart, "Metaphor as Illness," in *The Arms of the Windmill: Essays in Analytical Psychology in Honor of Werner H. Engel* (Baltimore: Lucas Printing Co., 1983), pp. 198-201.

26. See D.W. Winicott, *Playing and Reality* (London: Tavistock, 1971), pp. 89-90, 119, 136-137. See also Ann Belford Ul-

anov, *Receiving Woman: Studies in the Psychology and Theology of the Feminine* (Philadephia: Westminister, 1981), pp. 57-63. Many cover over even traumatic events with projection. A clinical example illustrates the process: Before one woman came into analytical treatment, she had suffered the trauma of rape. She knew perfectly well she had not in any way caused it, simply was not to blame. Nonetheless, she derived some comfort from interpreting the trauma in relation to what she called her failure to claim fully the power of her own authority in an incident just prior to the rape. She found herself in a bad summer job abroad, one that was both demeaning and depressing. So she quit and came home. She knew she had acted decisively here, out of her own authority. On arriving home, she accepted her lover's invitation to come to see him. But when she arrived, he fell into complaining about his wife and all his own problems. She thought to herself that she must end this nonsense or just get out. She was not there to be Mommy or therapist. But her firm resolve left her; she adapted herself to the nagging circumstances. Then, on her return home, came the rape. She found meaning, now, in connecting her letting go of the resolute power inside herself with the assault on her from the outside. Traumatic as the attack was, she felt finally she had rescued some meaning from it.

27. Joyce MacDougall, "Primitive Communication and the Use of Countertransference," in *Countertransference*, eds. Laurence Epstein and Arthur Feiver (Northvale N.J.: Jason Aronson, 1979), p. 270.

28. See Paul Ricoeur, *Freud and Philosophy: An Essay on Interpretation*, trans. Denis Savage (New Haven: Yale University Press, 1970), pp. 496-497. See also C.G. Jung, *Two Essays in Analytical Psychology*, *CW* 7, trans. R.F.C. Hull (New York: Pantheon, 1966), pp. 80-89, para. 121-140.

29. C.G. Jung, *Memories, Dreams, Reflections*, ed. Aniela Jaffé, trans. Richard and Clara Winston (New York: Pantheon, 1963), p. 297.

30. Paul Ricoeur, *The Symbolism of Evil*, trans. Emerson Buchanan (New York: Harper & Row, 1967), p. 314. Jung discusses

such suffering as experience of the dark side of God. See Jung, *Answer to Job*, *CW* 11, pp. 371, 411, 428, 430, 432ff, 450, 455; para. 572-573, 652, 685, 689, 693ff, 732, 739.

31. Paul Ricoeur, *Freud and Philosophy*, p. 549.
32. For discussion of the ego and the Self, see C.G. Jung, "The Ego" and "The Self," in *Aion*, *CW* 9:2, trans. R.F.C. Hull (New York: Pantheon, 1959), pp. 3-8, 23-36; para. 1-12, 43-67.
33. See Jung, *Alchemical Studies*, *CW* 13, pp. 89, 183, 295, 332; para. 118, 228, 19O, 446; see also, *The Herder Symbol Dictionary*, pp. 46, 173; see also, Russell A. Lockhart, "Coins and Psychological Change," in *Soul and Money*, (Dallas: *Spring*, 1982), pp. 25-25.
34. See Lockhart, "Coins and Psychological Change."
35. Ibid., p. 17.
36. Ibid., p. 22.
37. Marie-Louise von Franz, *Projection and Recollection in Jungian Psychology*, trans. William H. Kennedy (La Salle: Open Court, 1980), p. 177.
38. Lockhart, "Coins and Psychological Change," pp. 19-20.
39. Gerard Manley Hopkins, "The Blessed Virgin Compared to the Air we Breathe," in *Poems of Gerard Manley Hopkins*, ed. W.H. Gardner (New York: Oxford University Press, 1948), pp. 99-103.
The pertinent lines are:
> Wild air, world-mothering air,
> Nestling me everywhere,
> …
> I say that we are wound
> As if with air: the same
> Is Mary, more by name.
> She, wild web, wondrous robe,
> Mantles the guilty globe
> Since God Has let dispense
> Her prayers his providence:
> …
> She holds high motherhood
> Towards all our ghostly good

And plays in grace her part
About man's beating heart,
Laying, like air's fine flood,
the deathdance in his blood;
...
World-mothering air, air wild,
Wound with thee, in thee isled,
Fold home, fast fold thy child.

See also, Jung, *Psychology and Religion, CW* 11: "Blue is the colour of Mary's cloak: she is the earth covered by the blue tent of the sky. ... she represents the earth, which is also the body and its darkness." p. 71; par. 123.

40. Marie-Louise von Franz, *On Dreams and Death*, trans. Emmanuel Xipolitas Kennedy and Vernon Brooks (Boston: Shambhala, 1986), p. 89.

41. Jung, *Mysterium Coniunctionis, CW* 14, trans. R.F.C. Hull (New York: Pantheon, 1963), p. 494, par. 705. See also, Jung, *Psychology and Religion, CW* 11, p. 100; par. 160: The goal of alchemy "was to extract the original divine spirit out of chaos, and this extract was called the *quinta essentia, aqua permanens,* ύδωρ θειον, βαφη or tinctura. ... le ciel humain, the human sky or heaven. ... a blue liquid and incorruptible like the sky ... the colour of the sky...." and par. 161: "The miraculous liquid, the divine water, called sky or heaven, probably refers to the supra-celestial waters, of Genesis 1:7. In its functional aspect it was thought to be a sort of baptismal water which, like the holy water of the Church, possesses a creative and transformative quality."

42. Jung, *Mysterium Coniunctionis, CW* 14 , p. 763, para. 762.

43. *Ibid.*, p. 539, para. 770.

44. See C.G. Jung, *The Archetypes of the Collective Unconscious, CW,* 9:1, trans. R.F.C. Hull (New York: Pantheon, 1959), p. 146, para 256 where he describes Jerusalem as a Self symbol, and its connection to the experience of death: "... the self, enthroned in the place of the middle, and referred to in revelation as the beloved city (Jerusalem, the centre of the earth).... psychologically speaking, when individual con-

sciousness is extinguished in the waters of darkness, that is to say, when a *subjective* end of the world is experienced.... is meant the moment when consciousness sinks back into the darkness from which it originally emerged ... the moment of death."

45. Jung, *Letters*, Vol. II, p. 146, 1/25/54. The dream ends with this scene: "He has to go on a long climb ending at the edge of a deep precipice. A voice commands him to leap; after several desperate refusals, he obeys and finds himself swimming deliciously into the blue of eternity." Lest we think that such dreams turn up only in the practice of analysts, let me quote the report of a recurrent dream of a political figure, Lee Atwater, former chairman of the Republican National Committee: "I was jumping off a cliff into the ocean, but I always woke up before I hit the water." He understood his dream to mean this: "It was about my inability to make the leap of faith that was necessary to face mortality." After the discovery of his terminal illness from a brain tumor, Atwater apologized for the "naked cruelty" of some of his remarks during the presidential campaign of 1988. We might speculate that the recurring dream functions to make the dreamer "wake up" to "cruel" aspects of his behavior and set matters aright before he "hits the water." *The New York Times*, Sunday, January 13, 1991.

46. Soren Kierkegaard, *Concluding Unscientific Postscript*, trans. David F. Swenson and Walter Lowrie (Princeton: Princeton University Press, 1941), pp. 493-498, 507, 513, 516.

47. Nancy had two dreams featuring a robbery motif, in late April of 1985, that presaged the disaster about to befall her. (Her tumor was not diagnosed until October of that same year.) The dreams employ archetypal imagery of theft and expulsion to herald her coming death. The first dream was as follows: "I am in P's apartment [the man she would marry], but it is the reverse of life. Here his is on a higher floor than mine, whereas in real life mine is higher. I go down to my apartment, and it has been broken into. *All* my possessions – my clothes, my furniture, my photographs – everything was stolen, except for some Japanese prints and a

bedroom set my family gave me. Those items depress me; they are depressing, bleak and full of worry. I was robbed of all my personal things. It had a vampire-like quality, like a transfer of my things to someone else to organize their life. The life sucked out of you. It was a ruthless disregard of me as a subject, as a person, so opposed to a conscious view it is outlawed and can only break in. All my possessions were gone. I was dispossessed."

The second dream: "My apartment, not the one with P, but mine. The door is bulging. It might be going to blow up. There are flies or bees or hornets swarming out. It was somewhat dangerous and certainly not available to me anymore. I did not know what to do, but I couldn't go inside."

I worried about these dreams at the time and worried about them in retrospect, too. If I had insisted then that Nancy see a physician for a complete medical checkup, would the tumor have been discovered in time to prevent its fatal outcome? It is important to note that neither dream depicts Nancy as dead. It is only her former home that is no longer available to her – not her life.

At the time of these dreams, Nancy was exhausted, frantic with all that she had to do. She was fighting for a decent raise at work, planning her wedding, discovering that the caterer she had hired had just been diagnosed as having Hodgkin's disease but wanted to do the job anyway. She was making a decision about perhaps leaving her work in science, grappling with parents who seemed to her unresponsive to all the changes in her life. She was arranging to sell her apartment and trying to find a new one large enough for a married life.

We related the dreams' dramatic imagery to this current stress and to Nancy's earlier fear of marriage as a threat to her individuality. She had worked through this fear, but it did not seem strange at all recurring now, as it did, in the face of her forthcoming wedding with all its attendant details and preparations. Here, in the dreams, she loses her own particular apartment, which she was in fact giving up to move into her fiancé's place. What I failed to note strongly enough was the possibility that the death-marriage motif might apply to Nancy literally. We were unable at the time, either of us, to plumb the deeper meaning of the dream, which, looking back with the clarity of hindsight, now seems to have unmistakable foreshadowings about it. See von Franz, *On Dreams and Death*, Chapter 3.

48. For discussion of this level of mentation, see C.G. Jung, "Two Kinds of Thinking," in *Symbols of Transformation*, *CW* 5, trans. R.F.C. Hull (Princeton: Princeton University Press, 1974), pp. 7-33, para. 4-46; see also Ernst Cassirer, *Language and Myth*, trans. Suzanne K. Langer (New York: Harper & Brothers, 1969), pp. 1-23; see also Hans W. Loewald, *Psychoanalysis and the History of the Individual* (New Haven: Yale University Press, 1978), pp. 9, 12, 15, 19, 31, 56-57, 61; see also Nathan Schwartz-Salant, *The Borderline Personality, Vision and Healing* (Wilmette: Chiron, 1989), Chapter 5; see also Marion Milner, *On Not Being Able To Paint* (New York: International Universities Press, 1979), Chapters 1, 2, 5; see also James Hillman, *The Dream and the Underworld* (San Francisco: Harpers, 1979), Chapter I.

49. See Ann Belford Ulanov, "Needs, Wishes, and Transcendence," in *Picturing God*.

50. See Winnicott, *Playing and Reality*, pp. 72, 75, 80, 84; see also Harry Guthrip, *Schizoid Phenomena, Object Relations and the Self* (New York: International Universities Press, 1969), Chapter 9.

51. See Sigmund Freud, *The Ego and the Id*, trans. Joan Rivere and James Strachey (New York: Norton, 1960), pp. 21, 23; see also Sigmund Freud, *The Essays on the Theory of Sexuality*, *Standard Edition*, Vol. 7, trans. James Strachey (London: Hogarth Press, 1973), p. 220; see also Melanie Klein, *Envy and Gratitude and Other Works 1946-1963* (New York: Delacorte Press Seymour Lawrence, 1975), pp. 82, 135, 169, 306, 307.

52. See C.G. Jung, "Concerning the Archetypes, with Special Reference to the Anima Concept," *CW* 9:1 and C.G. Jung, "The syzygy: Anima and Animus," in *Aion: Researches into the Phenomenology of the Self*, *CW*, Vol. 9:2, trans. R.F.C. Hull

(New York: Pantheon, 1959) see also A. B. Ulanov, *The Feminine*, p. 334; see also Ann and Barry Ulanov, *The Witch and the Clown: Two Archetypes of Human Sexuality* (Wilmette: Chiron, 1987), pp. 152-159.

53. See A. B. Ulanov, *The Feminine*, pp. 184, 284, 328, 330.

54. See Evelyn Fox Keller, *Reflections on Gender and Science* (New Haven: Yale University Press, 1986), for discussion of science done in the masculine mode.

55. The feminine modes of thinking are not necessarily strong in all women nor necessarily stronger in women than in men. In some men this mode of being may be very strong. I have found in teaching graduate students that it is important to assess the predominant modes of each student's thinking as well as those of the group, and to adjust my presentation of material accordingly. What makes a class exciting is the mixture of predominant modes and the flexibility of approach it commands in all of us.

56. D.W. Winnicott, "Ego Distortion in Terms of True and False Self (1960)," in *The Maturational Processes and the Facilitating Environment* (New York: International Universities Press, 1965), pp. 142-144, 146, 148, 151.

57. See Paul Tillich, "The Eternal Now," in *The Eternal Now* (New York: Scribner's, 1963); see also Loewald, *Psychoanalysis and the History of the Individual*, pp. 62-70 for his discussion of the "eternal now."

58. D. W. Winnicott, "Living Creatively," in *Home Is Where We Start From*, eds., Clare Winnicott, Ray Shepherd, Madeleine Davis (New York: Norton, 1986); see also Winnicott, *Playing and Reality*, p. 100; see also Masud R. Khan, "The Finding and Becoming of Self," in *The Privacy of the Self* (New York: International Universities Press, 1974); see also Bernard Landis, "Discussions with Harry Guntrip," *Contemporary Psychoanalysis*, Vol., 17, No. 1, 1981, pp. 112-117; see also Heinz Kohut, *The Restoration of the Self* (New York: International Universities Press, 1977), pp. 310-311; see also Jung, *Letters*, I, p. 326, 12/22/42; see also Jung, *Memories, Dreams, Reflections*, p. 325.

59. In striking contrast to Nancy, there is the man to whom Jung writes, one who does not stick to his task, consciously engaging what confronts him and finding its meaning: "The fight takes place there in the unconscious because it doesn't take place in your consciousness. It forms a tail-devouring *Ouroboros* to the exclusion of yourself, and that's the reason why you are still a baby and have such a huge anima on account of it." *Letters,* I, p. 463, 5/20/47.

60. I am indebted to Nancy's husband for permission to make slides and prints of Nancy's paintings and for cataloguing and dating the originals.

61. Jung, *Letters,* I, pp. 169-170, 7/23/34; see also *The Herder Dictionary of Symbols,* p. 21 and J. C. Cooper, *An Illustrated Encyclopedia of Traditional Symbols* (London: Thames and Hudson, 1978), pp. 19-20, both of which remind us that the bee was a royal symbol in Chaldea and in imperial France, a symbol of the soul in Egypt, and in ancient Greece was associated with the priestesses of Eleusis and Ephesus. In Celtic tradition, the bee stands for a secret wisdom coming from the other world. In Christian symbolism, the bee represents hope, good order, purity, courage. For Bernard of Clairvaux, the bee stands for the Holy Ghost; it was also associated with the Christ figure and the Immaculate Conception of the Virgin Mary.

62. Gold was the only metal the ancients knew that did not corrode with age or acid; for many it still carries projections of immortality and eternity, and remains, as a substance of the highest value, the standard of choice for monetary systems. Gold is associated for most people with the sun and with almost everything of superior quality and does constant service as such in our rhetoric. Silver, as we have seen, is connected to purity, lunar light, and the feminine principle.

63. Aniela Jaffé writes of Jung telling one of his last dreams, in which such darkness figured so centrally. She writes: "His expression was distant, his voice very soft ... and he interrupted the narrative several times with long periods of silence, as if he were once more immersed in that colossal

'expanse,' 'dark distance and strangeness' that appears to characterize the borders between reality and the transcendent, between consciousness and the unconscious." She quotes Jung: "A dark distance. It stretches into the infinite...." (p. 114) "There is an unbelievable width and depth of space before me. And the darkness!" (p. 115) "It was dark, the beginning of night, or rather, a night-like darkness, and space of monstrous breadth, an emptiness, a colossal emptiness." (p. 116) " I have the feeling that ... my tiredness during the last few days is connected with this dream experience, with this enormous distance from which I had to return. I have the feeling of a great task: I must return, must reduce the distance." (p. 117) Aniela Jaffé, *Was C.G. Jung a Mystic?* trans. Diana Dachler and Fiona Cairns (Einsiedeln: Daimon Verlag, 1989).

See also Jung's own words about facing death: "Yet death is an important interest, especially to an aging person. A categorical question is being put to him, and he is under obligation to answer it. To this end he ought to have a myth about death, for reason shows him nothing but the dark pit into which he is descending. Myth, however, can conjure up other images for him, helpful and enriching pictures of life in the land of the dead. If he believes in them, or greets them with some measure of credence, he is being just as right or just as wrong as someone who does not believe in them. But while the man who despairs marches toward nothingness, the one who has placed his faith in the archetype follows the tracks of life and lives right into his death. Both, to be sure, remain in uncertainty, but the one lives against his instincts, the other with them." Jung, *Memories, Dreams, Reflections*, p. 306.

64. See Ann and Barry Ulanov, *The Healing Imagination, The Meeting of Psyche and Soul* (Mahwah: Paulist, 1991), Chapter 1.
65. Blessed John Ruysbroeck, "The Book of the Sparkling Stone," in *Medieval Netherlands Religious Literature*, trans. Edmund Colledge (London: Heinemann, 1965), p. 95.
66. D.W. Winnicott, *Human Nature* (London: Free Association Books, 1988), p. 78.

67. For discussion of resurrection as a psychic image, see G. Mogenson, "The Resurrection of the Dead: A Jungian Approach to the Mourning Process," *Journal of Analytical Psychology*, 35, 3, 1990. Death punctuates the sentence of our lives. If we do not engage the resurrection image, death is like a fullstop period; if we do engage the image, it is a startled exclamation point!

68. Jung says of his own experience "... in the blackest night even, and just there, by the grace of God, I could see a Great Light. Somewhere there seems to be great kindness in the abysmal darkness of the deity...." Gerhard Adler, "Personal Encounters with Jung and His Work," in *Dynamics of the Self* (London: Coventure, 1979) p. 90.

69. von Franz, *On Dreams and Death*, pp. 61-62.

70. *Ibid.*, p. 60. Three years after this picture of Nancy's of 5/86, on 6/89 – which was two years after her death – I dreamt of this image and in the dream likened it to Nancy's drawing, though in my dream the hole in the center was bigger and not in color.

71. For a discussion of "immediate experience" see C.G. Jung, *Psychology and Religion*, in *Psychology and Religion: West and East*, *CW* 11, p. 43, para. 75.

72. Jung, *Memories, Dreams, Reflections*, p. 335.

73. *Ibid.*, p. 335n, added by Aniela Jaffé.

74. C.G. Jung, *The Transcendent Function,* 'in *CW* 8; see also Jung, *Mysterium Coniunctionis*, *CW* 14, pp. 200, 202, 494; para. 259, 261, 705ff.

75. *Ibid.*, p. 546, para. 778: "The ego never lacks moral and rational counterarguments, which one cannot and should not set aside so long as it is possible to hold on to them. For you only feel yourself on the right road when the conflicts of duty seem to have resolved themselves, and you have become the victim of a decision made over your head or in defiance of the heart. From this we can see the numinous power of the self, which can hardly be experienced in any other way. For this reason *the experience of the self is always a defeat for the ego*. The extraordinary difficulty in this experience is that the self can be distinguished only conceptually

from what has always been referred to as 'God,' but not practically."

76. The mystical body, the glorified body and the resurrection body are instinct in Christian tradition with community and are fed by the sacraments. The subtle body, a related but not identical notion from alchemy, is fed by the conscious exercise of the ego in relation to Self. Consciousness does not equal reasoning, but rather stands for self-awareness in perception and apperception. For discussion of these ideas, see Ann and Barry Ulanov, *The Healing Imagination*, pp. 146ff.

77. For discussion of countertransference, see Ann Belford Ulanov, "Follow-Up Treatment in Cases of Patient-Therapist Sex," in *Journal of the American Academy of Psychoanalysis*, 1979, 7, 1, pp. 101-110; see also Ann Belford Ulanov, "Transference / Countertransference: A Jungian Perspective," in *Jungian Analysis*, ed. Murray Stein (La Salle: Open Court, 1982).

78. Jung, *Letters*, I, p. 270, 5/22/39.

79. *Ibid.*, p. 239, 12/1/37.

80. Dorothy M. Emmet, *The Nature of Metaphysical Thinking* (London: MacMillan, 1957), p. 105; see also Ann and Barry Ulanov, "Reaching to the Unknown," in *Clinical Handbook of Pastoral Counseling*, Vol. 2: current issues, ed. Robert J. Wicks (Mahwah: Paulist, 1992).

81. See Ann Belford Ulanov, "Disguises of the Anima," in *Gender and Soul in Psychotherapy*, eds. Nathan Schwartz-Salant and Murray Stein, *The Chiron Clinical Series* (Wilmette: Chiron, 1992); see also A.B. Ulanov, "Transference / Countertransference," in *Jungian Analysis*.

82. I dreamt of Nancy several times. One early dream came after seeing Nancy in the hospital with a big, crescent scar on her head, from her first brain operation. I dreamt I was unable to hold together a class I was teaching or keep hold of the subject matter. I just let it all go. A student holds me as I weep for Nancy. In a late dream, a month before Nancy's death, she appeared as her old thin self, lively, eating applesauce with pleasure. This dream came after the idea arrived to do something radically different with her sessions

(see p. 99); that was my association to applesauce, which is something I make from my own recipe.

83. Heinz Kohut, *The Restoration of the Self* (New York: International Universities Press, 1979), pp. 187n, 188n; see also Heinz Kohut, *How Does Analysis Cure?* (Chicago: University of Chicago Press, 1984), pp. 48-50; see also Robert D. Stolorow, Bernard Brandschaft and George Atwood, *Psychoanalytic Treatment, An Intersubjective Approach* (Hillsdale: The Analytic Press, 1987), Chapter 5.

84. Simone Weil, *Waiting for God*, trans. Emma Craufurd (New York: Putnam's, 1951), p. 115.

85. T.S. Eliot, "Burnt Norton," *The Four Quartets* in *The Complete Poems and Plays* (New York: Harcourt, Brace & Co., 1952), p. 121.

86. Melanie Klein, "A Contribution to the Psychogenesis of Manic-Depressive States" and "Mourning and Its Relation to Manic-Depressive States," and "The Oedipus Complex in the Light of Early Anxieties" in Melanie Klein, *Love, Guilt and Reparation and Other Works 1921-1945* (New York: Delacorte Press Seymour Lawrence, 1975).

87. See C.G. Jung, "Synchronicity: An Acausal Connecting Principle" in *The Structure and Dynamics of the Psyche, CW* 8, pp. 417-533, para. 7; see also Robert Aziz, *C.G. Jung's Psychology of Religion and Synchronicity* (Albany: SUNY, 1990).

88. For discussion of religious experience reaching us through the feminine mode of being, see Ann Belford Ulanov, *The Wisdom of the Psyche*, p. 135.

Index

Susan Bach
Life Paints its Own Span
*On the Significance of
Spontaneous Paintings by
Severely Ill Children*
with over 200 color illustrations
Part I (Text): 208 pages
Part II (Pictures): 56 pgs.
ISBN 3-85630-516-5

This pioneering work, with over 200 color reproductions, is a comprehensive exposition of Susan Bach's original approach to the physical and psychospiritual evaluation of spontaneous paintings and drawings by severely ill patients. At the same time, this work is a moving record of Susan Bach's own journey of discovery.

The latest Jungian Congress Proceedings:

Chicago 1992
*The Transcendent Function:
Individual and Collective Aspects
edited by Mary Ann Mattoon*
560 pages, illustrated
ISBN 3-85630-538-6 (paperback)
ISBN 3-85630-537-8 (hardbound)

The Twelfth International Congress for Analytical Psychology was held in Chicago from August 23-28,1992. Some sixty presentations were made by Jungian analysts from around the world, and they appear in their entirety in this volume. Some selections from the contents: "The Transcendent Function in Therapy after Incestuous Violence" by Petra Affeld-Niemeyer with a response by Betty De Shong Meador, "Psychodrama and the Transcendent Function" by Helmut Barz, "Decoding the Diamond Body: The Structure of the Self and the Transcendent Function" by Robert Moore, "Analytical Psychology and Politics" by Andrew Samuels.

A Festschrift for Sir Laurens van der Post:

The Rock Rabbit and the Rainbow

edited by Robert Hinshaw

ca. 200 pages, illustrated
ISBN 3-85630-540-8 (paper)
ISBN 3-85630-512-2 (hardbound)

Authors from around the world have combined their talents in a tribute honoring this writer, soldier, statesman and man of his time. Contributions include: Joseph Henderson: "The Splendor of the Sun"; Alan McGlashan: "How to be Haveable"; Ian Player: "My Friend Nkunzimlanga"; Jean-Marc Pottiez: "Rainbow Rhapsody"; T.C. Robertson: "A Triad of Landscapes – a Day in the Veld with Laurens"; and numerous other essays and works by Aniela Jaffé, Jonathan Stedall, Harry Wilmer, Jo Wheelright, C.A. Meier and many others.

Alan McGlashan
Gravity & Levity
The Philosophy of Paradox
ca. 200 pages, illustrated
ISBN 3-85630-548-3

This book heralds a breakthrough in human imagination. Not a breakthrough that may take place in the future, far or near, but one that has already occurred – we just may not have noticed it. Life, as the author shows it, is "open-ended" and full of paradoxes. Its principles cannot be understood by logic and causal reasoning. What is needed, he suggests, is not merely an uneasy recognition but a joyous acceptance that reality cannot be other than paradoxical.

"One of the most important books that has come my way for many years ... He is that rare phenomenon among men, one able to detect the movement of the spirit that could rid us of a crippling sense of meaninglessness and loss of purpose." – Laurens van der Post